Richard Davies

Leaves from the history of Welsh nonconformity in the seventeenth century

Richard Davies

Leaves from the history of Welsh nonconformity in the seventeenth century

ISBN/EAN: 9783337113803

Printed in Europe, USA, Canada, Australia, Japan

Cover: Foto ©ninafisch / pixelio.de

More available books at **www.hansebooks.com**

LEAVES

FROM THE

HISTORY OF

WELSH NONCONFORMITY

IN THE

SEVENTEENTH CENTURY.

Being chiefly the Autobiography of Richard Davies
of Welshpool—Quaker. (1636-1708.)

EDITED BY
JOHN E. SOUTHALL.

NEWPORT, MON.
J. E. SOUTHALL, PRINTER AND PUBLISHER.
1899.

NOTE.

The spelling Welch-pool, follows the English edition of 1825.

PREFACE.

The accompanying Autobiography has been in the main a reprint of the sixth English edition of 1825; the notes are almost wholly fresh matter, and some explanatory paragraphs are interspersed in the text. These may be recognised by the distance between the lines being slightly wider. In 1840, a Welsh edition was issued with the following title : " Hanes arghoeddiad, trafferthion gwasanaeth a theithiau yr hen was hwnw o eiddo yr Arglwydd, Richard Davies, yn cynnwys peth hanes am daeniad y gwirionedd yn Ngogledd Cymru wedi ei gyfieithu o'r chweched argraffiad yn Saesoneg." The few remaining copies of the edition were given away by the Recording Clerk of the modern Society of Friends about 1893, so that it is not now in print.

I may say, that, in issuing an eighth edition (the seventh English edition appeared in 1840) I have not sought to simply present an interesting piece of literature for the antiquarian. The importance of the subject matter lies in a different direction, yet I cannot expect the work to be fully valued by the general public on those grounds. It is only those who share Richard Davies' religious convictions, and who would have to act to-day as he acted were they in similar circumstances, who will appreciate to the full the beauty and consistency of the worship, life and conversation he was concerned to promote both by example and word of mouth.

This journal appears to have been written in English, and it may be doubted whether R. D. possessed the capacity to *write* freely in the language of the country, which must have been the usual medium of communication at religious meetings in Montgomery and Merioneth at that time, and one frequently used by himself in preaching. It is probable that the successive English editions found their way into Wales only to a very small extent; so far as I am aware, none of the prominent Welsh Methodists of the last century had ever heard of the work. It is now however more widely known, especially in Powysland, and some notice of it appeared not very long ago, in the "London Kelt."

There is now no meeting held in Wales or its borders, corresponding to those of the Primitive Quakers; there are, however, several in South Wales and Herefordshire, under the care of the Society which is usually credited with the Quaker name and with carrying on their work. In the matter of religion, names go for very little; when a Church calls itself Catholic and Apostolic, we look for proof of Catholicity, and for a manifestation of the same essential fruits of Christianity as characterized Apostolic times, just so, when any name with commanding greatness is introduced to characterize a set of doctrines or a profession of Christianity, it is the duty of all honest seekers after Truth to take nothing upon trust. In fact it was never the intention of its Divine founder that Christianity should be propagated on those conditions. "He that is of God heareth us, said the Apostle, and he that is not of God heareth us not."

The best work of the last half of the 17th century was entitled by one who participated in it to be, "Primitive Christianity revived," and its claims to-day rest on the assent of the enlightened spiritual understanding. He that is of God—*i.e.*, he whose spiritual ears are Divinely opened, hears those early testimonies and honours them, so to-day, he that is not of God, or is ruled by the wisdom that is from beneath not from above, may seem to assent; but those that are actuated by it have no true knowledge, no true faith,—they do not hear aright.

So there may be those now drawn by the inward Witness for Truth to livingly receive somewhat of true faith as to Gospel worship, and desirous of finding such as hold meetings in the same faith as Richard Davies and his friends. If such come in contact with Societies or meetings where a profession of it is made, but find that the ground or foundation is in reality that of the Independents from whom R. D. came out, and which is substantially the same in all the prominent sects to-day, let not these conclude that spiritual worship is either an empty phrase or as much at the command of the creature as singing a hymn in a so-called Evangelistic meeting.

In other words, if any reading these pages attend the meetings attached to the modern Society of Friends, &c., in the hope of finding them held in the same power and authority as the gatherings of faithful friends of the 17th century, and if such are disappointed, let them not conclude that the same faith, the same power, and the same heavenly results will be withheld even in these days where sought aright in the "silence of all flesh," Hab. ii. 20., Zech. ii. 13., nor let them suppose that the mere profession of worship in the Spirit brings the reality along with it.

Wales needs many things, but nothing more than a thorough reformation in religion, a reformation which will strike a fatal blow at the pretensions of all those, whether prelatical or dissenting, who attempt to walk off with the keys of the kingdom of heaven in their pocket, a reformation which makes the right shoulders feel the responsibilities of life for time and for eternity, and which will cleanse the inward temple from the idols of silver and gold, a reformation which replaces the double-minded hypocrisy of trying to extract the greatest amount of pleasure out of both worlds, by a willing compliance with the requirements of the straight gate and the narrow way as inwardly manifested, even when the intoxication of sweet sounds and voices has to be denied and turned from, that the ear may be attuned to better harmonies :* a reformation in fact that will bring people to sit under the teachings and heavenly operations of the everlasting Gospel, which was the only means of salvation before Matthew, Mark, Luke, and John were written, is now, unchangeably the same, and is NOT WORDS, but the POWER, and the only *sure foundation* of religion.

It is for the benefit of those who sigh for such a reformation that this account of Richard Davies' exercises and stedfastness is offered to view. It is the editor's faith that there will be such a reformation in Wales, though at present, the signs are rather the other way, even among most of the professed representatives of the principles of the Early Friends. Its nature is prophetically foreshadowed in the following extract from a sermon by Sarah Grubb, delivered in London in 1821.

"I see a day with my spiritual eye wherein, whether we are faithful or not, there shall be a people preserved who shall then exalt the Lord's power *alone*, they shall assemble and sit down in silence, in awful and reverent stillness; they shall wait for the arising of life and the power of Christ among them to a greater extent than has yet prevailed, and they shall be each others' crown, and rejoicing in Christ. They shall maintain this testimony until the coming of that glorious gospel day "when the earth shall be full of the knowledge of the Lord, as the waters cover the sea."

6 mo. 1899. J. E. S.

*It may not be generally known that from the dispensation of Light and Grace into which Richard Davies and the early Friends were called, instrumental music and hymn singing in the will of man, was excluded both in meetings and the family circle.

CONTENTS.

CHAPTER I.

Nonconformity in Wales during the first half of the Seventeenth Century, of indigenous origin, yet nurtured from England 1

CHAPTER II.

Birth, early life, and convincement ... 8

CHAPTER III.

Piercing power in a Silent Meeting at Shrewsbury—Visit to a gay company of dancers—Roger Prichard—Vavasor Powell—Meetings in the open-air decided on—Goes to London—Inward pointings toward marriage—Meets George Fox—Imprisoned at Montgomery and Shrewsbury, Bridgenorth ... 31

CHAPTER IV.

A Meeting at Dolobran—Lord Herbert of Chirbury—Charles Lloyd Imprisoned—Letter to the Quarter Sessions—Truth spreading in Merioneth—Vavasor Powell's Lament—James Parkes Addresses Professors at Wrexham—Richard Davies's Testimony at the Steeple House—The Hireling Flies 56

CHAPTER V.

The schism of John Perrot—Richard Davies burdened with unanointed Preaching—Testimony against Cadwalader Edwards—Meeting at Aberystwith and Imprisonment of Richard Davies—Journey with John ap John—Roger Prichard restored—French Bretons—Cardiff—The vile Informer 87

CHAPTER VI.

Persecution in Merionethshire—Price of Rhiwlas and Salisbury of Rûg—D. Maurice an Informer—His miserable end—George Fox a Prisoner—Counsellor Corbet gets him clear at Westminster Hall—Threat of Counsellor Walcott—Lord Powis—Oppression of Ludlow Court of Marches—Priest outwitted—Yearly-Meeting for Wales settled ... 110

CHAPTER VII.

Bishop of Asaph tries to get Dissenters into his fold—Reasons why Quakers Dissent—R. D. denies the term Lord Bishop and interviews the Bishop—Sir Lionel Jenkin, Secretary of State—False Brethren—Outlines of Sermon—Insulted by Queen's Lifeguards in 1683. 127

CHAPTER VIII.

R. D., by means of inward grace and discernment, detects a Jesuit preaching as a Quaker—Renewed persecution for absence from the corrupt national worship—The declaration of indulgence—Coming in of the Prince of Orange—Kindness of the then Bishop of Asaph—Scholars at Oxford attend Meeting in 1700 ... 143

CHAPTER IX.

Appointed to meet Queen Anne at Windsor—The Scholars at Oxford manifest some improvement—Attends Yearly Meeting at London—Last illness and Death—Testimony of George Whitehead and of the Quarterly Meeting 159

CHAPTER I.

NONCONFORMITY IN WALES DURING THE FIRST HALF OF
THE SEVENTEENTH CENTURY OF INDIGENOUS ORIGIN,
YET NURTURED FROM ENGLAND.

NONCONFORMITY in Wales during the first half of the seventeenth century was chiefly confined to the Eastern portion of the country. Greater proximity to England does not wholly explain this, for a careful examination of history, reveals the fact that this early nonconformity was indigenous, and not simply the result of an English movement permeating Wales.

The interchange of ideas in West Wales was slow, the natural tendency of the people was conservative, and the Welsh language had not acquired the momentum which characterized it in the corresponding period of the nineteenth century, and which even such meagre opportunities of literary cultivation as existed from 1800 to 1850, imparted to it.

The art of printing, which was slowly but surely effecting such mighty changes in England, had, as yet, made but little impression upon Welsh Wales.

Hence it was, that the pioneers of Welsh nonconformity were largely dependent on the English press for information on the controversies of the day, and for such religious literature, as was then current. They appear to have been, almost all of them, bilingual speakers; they lived among people, very few of whom could read the native language, and nearly everything original, they published was in English—Morgan Llwyd, of Wrexham, being a notable exception.

Welsh nonconformity of the seventeenth century did not lay the foundation of a national literature; never very strong in comparison with the total population, its influence rather declined than increased, until well on into the eighteenth century, when something like a system of popular education, hand in hand with the religious movement associated with the names of Howell Harris, Rowlands of Llangeitho, and Williams of Pantycelyn, gave to the mass of the people a leverage for social, moral, and literary improvement which the Established Church was unable or unwilling to supply.

As a matter of fact, there is more parallelism existing between the history of popular literature in England and Wales than appears at first sight,—in each case the familiarity with the Bible preceded the spread of any literature which was current in any considerable section of the people at large. Popular literature was at first almost exclusively religious, and afterwards largely partook of the periodical character as is the case at the present day both in England and Wales.

In the fifteenth century there is ground for believing that Welsh literature was more abundant, head for head of the population than was the case with English literature, but neither preserved a truly popular character.

I am not classing the writings of Shakespeare, Spenser, Milton, and Dryden as popular literature; their writings had comparatively little influence on the average men and women of the seventeenth century: the era of popular literature in England, beyond that of a directly religious character, hardly began before the appearance of the "Spectator" and the "Tatler."

On the other hand, in Wales, though Gweirydd ap Rhys enumerates over 220 Welsh authors who were born in the 16th century, or who died between 1529 and 1600, and 51 men who were born in the seventeenth century before 1635,* no considerable body of popular literature was created by them; a large proportion of the bardic productions remained in manuscript, and some are in manuscript to this day.

The power of the press could not make headway against the governmental neglect of the national language, the poverty of the country, and the difficulties of intercommunication. Such works as the Martin Mar Prelate tracts could hardly obtain a circulation in Welsh, for the conditions were not favourable to the spread of new ideas, except where a knowledge of the English language was to be found.

The Bible itself was not so generally accessible as in England, but there were popular works, however, such as Llyfr y Ficer; in some instances there was probably a local, rather than a national popular literature, and the writings of Huw Morris, with other more obscure writers, may have occupied such a position; but a body of Welsh literature that may be justly styled popular, is the work of the present century, and was largely the fruit of the spread of denominational periodicals, and, indirectly, of the revival of the Eisteddfod.

---

* See " Hanes Llenyddiaeth Gymreig," published by *Foulkes, Liverpool.*

In the period which is to come under our notice, popular education had not, it is true, found a home in England, but the civil and religious movements of the times made such a call on the printing press, that the leaders of Nonconformity in Wales, and the sympathizers with the Parliamentary party generally, had strong incentives to apply to English sources for information, and come under the influence of English ideas, but they did not and could not Anglicize the country. Another century intervened, and then it seemed as if Wales had a new lease of national life, and it developed afresh, literary characteristics of its own, side by side with an advancing civilization. The development was imperfect, and the culture uneven, we grant; could it be otherwise under the domination of an alien race, an alien tongue, and an alien system of education? Yet for all that, it had, side by side with its weaknesses, remarkable, if not unique excellencies, scarcely yet understood by the English public.

I mention these things not because they directly bear upon my subject, but they help to shew what Welsh nonconformity in the seventeenth century was, and what it was not, in its relation to the intellectual activities of the nation; they are, however, side issues only, yet interwoven with the history of the days we are living in; in the following pages, we are mostly concerned with those facts which sprang directly from spiritual, not secular, causes.

The Reformation in Europe was only a gradual work; breaking with the Church of Rome was one thing, coming fully under the teaching of the Spirit and discarding merely human authority in religion was quite another. The first has a negative character only, the latter or true Reformation has a positive base from which all its negative positions proceed.

In Wales we see this principle illustrated fully, a breaking with Rome almost of necessity, rather than from conviction, and the adoption of a form of religion approved by the secular power; then we see signs of a real religious awakening, and of the consciousness of the spiritual need for a further reformation and of greater freedom for the teaching of the Spirit—I refer to the days of the Puritans—then we see here and there, the need realized in small congregations up and down the country, who not merely refused to be trammelled by the national religion, but who felt that every act of worship performed without Divine leading, rather hindered than helped their realization of the power and presence of God, which, above all, they sought unto.

Now, it very often happened that those who embraced this dispensation of the Spirit, and who were known by the name of Quakers, had been associated with that degree of Reformation which advanced beyond the Episcopal forms, though but partially, and was connected with the name of Puritan, and this happened far too often, for us to suppose that it was the effect of chance.

Just in those districts where we know that the most eminent and enlightened Puritans laboured previous to 1650, we find, with little exception, that congregations of the people called Quakers took root.

In Monmouthshire, the pious William Wroth, who, next to John Penry, may be called the morning star of the Puritan Reformation, laboured at Llanvaches, and was deprived of his living during the primacy of Archbishop Laud. There was never a Quaker congregation at Llanvaches, but we may fairly assign to a probable connection with his work, the establishment of a meeting in the neighbouring village of Shirenewton, and it may be that even Pontymoyle meeting owed its rise to his influence.

William Erbery, priest of Mary's, Cardiff, refused to read the Book of Sports, that is to say, he may be classed as a Puritan; he was ejected, and his wife became a Quaker,* one of the very first of that profession in the town. As for Erbery himself, Rees, the author of the "History of Protestant Nonconformity in Wales," says that his views of the ministry and ordinances were similar to those of the Quakers.

Another Puritan preacher, Walter Cradock, who, likewise, had been ejected at Cardiff for refusal to read the Book of Sports, was protected and encouraged by Sir Robert Harley, at Brampton Bryan, on the borders of Radnorshire, and made preaching excursions into that county, where afterwards George Fox had a meeting, "like a leaguer [a camp] for multitudes," in 1657. He stood on a chair about three hours, and "all were bowed under the power of God."

Coming northwards, we can easily glean from Richard Davies' autobiography, that his position as hearer of Vavasor Powell at Welshpool was a stepping stone to his taking a stand in religious matters independently of

---

* This is on the authority of Rees.

the existing congregations, which was equivalent to his entering on a further degree of reformation.

Further north still, the same principle is illustrated at Wrexham, where it would appear that the labours of Walter Cradock and Morgan Llwyd paved the way for a gathering of worshippers, who, in the words of holy writ, were made 'wiser than their teachers.'

We know that John ap John one of Morgan Llwyd's hearers became an eminent Quaker preacher in the Welsh language, and we may justly infer that those he associated with in the Quaker profession near Wrexham, had been moulded in their earlier days after Puritan ideas.

The period at which the early Friends made their appearance was a stormy and unsettled one, both in a political, social, and religious sense. Welshpool, not far from the English border, was more than some other towns in Wales exposed to those influences, and they made their mark upon Richard Davies' life while he was yet a youth, but like most other Quaker autobiographers, he rarely goes out of his way to write history. The Vavasor Powell mentioned above was a noted man in his time; he was a native of Knucklas, in Radnorshire, and afterwards kept school at Clun, in Shropshire. His position as a Puritan caused him to leave Wales about the time of the outbreak of the Civil Wars, and he eventually became one of Commissioners to carry out the "Act for the Propagation of the Gospel in Wales," and was seldom two days a week without preaching.

He died in prison in 1670 after being confined, with only a short intermission, about 10 years, and was buried in Bunhill fields, London.

CHAPTER II.

RICHARD DAVIES, HIS BIRTH, EARLY LIFE, AND
CONVINCEMENT.

I WAS born in the year 1635, in the town of Welch-Pool, in Montgomeryshire, in North Wales, of honest parents, that had a small estate there: I was brought up in a little learning, and in the religion and discipline of the church of England. When I came to be about twelve or thirteen years of age, the Lord put his fear in my heart, that I came to a consideration, if I should die what would become of my soul, if I lived after the way that some of my companions did: and it came into my heart to leave them; and I was inclined to go and hear sermons, and followed the best of those sort of people, that I did believe feared the Lord, which I then thought were the Independent people; especially one Vavasor Powell, who was a very zealous man in his day and time; he took much pains and labour to gather a people into that persuasion, and many were gathered in these parts to that way; and I followed them from one parish to another, writing their sermons, and in time I came to repeat them to the people; and there, being exercised in the historical part of the scriptures, I could speak and talk of them, so that those people came to speak well of me, and this did not a little puff me up; so that I was not so serious, as I should have been, to get eternal life by Christ Jesus, who is the Life himself, who said to the Jews, John v. 39, 40. " Search, or ye search the Scriptures, for in them ye think to have eternal life, and they are they which testify of me: and ye will not come to me, that ye might have life."

We were diligent in searching the scriptures, which was good in its place; but the main matter and substance of pure religion, is the enjoyment of eternal life to the soul from Christ.

About the fourteenth year of my age, my father intended to put me apprentice to a shop-keeper, where I was for a trial: but I saw that the conversation of my intended master was not right, and that the fear of the Lord was not there. I was afraid, if I should continue there, that the little love and zeal I had to God and goodness, would be choked and quenched in me, and the love and pleasure of the world would get up again, so I should be in danger of growing worse than ever; and being under these serious considerations, I heartily prayed to God with tenderness and tears, what he put in my heart to pray for, viz., that I might be delivered from that place where I was intended to be bound an apprentice, and that I might spend my time with and amongst them that feared the Lord, and thought upon his name; and the Lord heard my prayers, and in a little time I was sent for, away from that place.

After this I staid at home some time, and continued in that little well-doing I had known, keeping company with sober and honest people; I delighted to read the scriptures, and to go to the Independent meetings. And after some time, I heard of a man that professed the same religion, who was very zealous for a time in going to meeting, and performing that which we call family duties, and there, with the consent of my parents, I bound myself an apprentice to him, whose name was Evan Jones, a felt-maker, in the parish of Llanfair, in Montgomeryshire; and we went together to meetings, I writing and repeating sermons, and performing that custom that was among us, in praying in our own will and time, till we were become so dead and formal, carnal and airy, many loose words and actions growing up amongst us, that I was gone out of conceit with myself, and our formal religion; there being something in me that reproved me for my vanity; and when I rose from my prayers, being some time in a weighty, ponderous condition, I saw that there was something that gave me no true peace nor comfort inwardly to my soul, because there remained a secret pride and self-exaltation in most, if not all, our formal performances.

In this state and condition I knew not what to do; when neither writing, repeating sermons, reading of the scriptures, and other good books, and sometimes expounding of them to the best of my understanding, afforded me any comfort, I was at a loss, and knew not what way to take, that I might have peace and comfort in my performances. Hitherto I knew not the Holy Spirit of the Lord, as I ought to have done, to be my leader and guide into all things that were necessary to my eternal salvation.

Upon a certain time we had a meeting at Hugh David's, a tenant of Charles Lloyd's, of Dolobran, where one of our Independent teachers, who was a great scripturian, was preaching, and I wrote after him; and in his sermon he said, "The time would come that there would be no need of the scriptures, any more than another book;" at which I very much stumbled; and after the meeting I asked him, When would that time be? He said, when the Lord would make a new covenant with his people, as is said in Jeremiah xxxi. 33, 34. "I will make a new covenant with the house of Israel; after those days, saith the Lord, I will put my law in their inward parts, and write it in their hearts, and will be their God, and they shall be my people. And they shall tell no more every man his neighbour, and every man his brother, saying, Know the Lord; for they shall all know me, from the least of them to the greatest of them, saith the Lord; for I will forgive their iniquity, and I will remember their sin no more." It seems that he knew not that day had come then, though he was a great preacher. I thought it would then be a happy day, when God would be the teacher of his people himself; that we need not teach every man his neighbour, or his brother, saying, "Know ye the Lord;" but that we should all know him, from the least to the greatest. This day we knew not then, for all our preaching and long prayers; though the Lord did then beget true hungerings and thirstings in our souls after him. We had great love and zeal, and desired the knowledge of the truth as is was in Jesus. Sometimes I have said, this was but like Jacob's dream, when he awoke and said, "Surely the Lord is in this place, and I knew it not." And indeed we knew not the Lord, as we ought to have done; namely, by his light, grace, and spirit shining in our hearts, to give us the light of the knowledge of the Son of God, which knowledge keeps a man meek and humble; and such are not puffed up in a vain mind, to seek after those things that are too high for them, as too many are climbing up that way, which is not the way to God the Father; the way to the Father is the way of holiness and purity, and humility, without which no man shall see the Lord, nor enjoy his presence to their comfort.

About this time, being in the year 1656, our ministers told us, that there was a sort of people come up in the north,* called Quakers, that were a people of a strange

---

* Truth arose powerfully in the northern parts of England in the year 1652.

posture and principles: saying, that it was the last days and times that Christ spoke of in the xxivth of Matthew, "Many shall come in my name, and deceive many, *ver.* 5. for there shall arise false christs, and false prophets, and shall shew great signs and wonders, insomuch that, if it were possible, they shall deceive the very elect." This sort of people called Quakers, were much preached against; they told us they were the false prophets, &c., that they denied the scriptures, and all ordinances, and also denied the very Christ that bought them. They were represented to us to be such a dangerous sort of people, that we were afraid of any who had the name of a Quaker, lest we should be deceived by them. Hitherto they had not been in these parts of the country, neither did we know what were the principles held out by themselves; but only such as were reported, though falsely, unto us by our preachers and others; which kept us in blindness, and from making further inquiry, and "trying all things, and holding fast that which is good," according to the apostle's advice, 1 Thes. v. 21.

Now about the year 1657, there came a poor man in a mean habit to my master's house, named Morgan Evan, of South-Wales: he had met with the people called Quakers in his travels, and was convinced of the truth. This poor man discoursed with my master about the principles of truth, and I being in the shop about my calling. my mistress came and said, why do you not go out to help your master? for there is a Quaker at the door that hath put him to silence. I hearing this, made haste, and took my bible under my arm, and put on what courage I could, to dispute with that poor man, but he proved too hard for us all; when I went to them, they were upon the words *Thee* and *Thou*; but I very peremptorily asked him, What command had he to speak *Thee* and *Thou;* for I did acknowledge to him, that it was the language of God to Adam, and the language of the scripture; but, said I, that is not enough for us now in this day, we must have a command for it. To which he answered, "Hold fast the form of sound words, which thou hast heard of me." I asked him, whether that was scripture; he asked me, whether I would deny it; I told him, he was to prove it. Then he took the bible out of my hand, and he turned to 2 Tim. i. 13, which he read, and told me, that *Hold fast* there, was a command; which I knew very well, both the scripture and the command: but to prove him further, I desired him to read a little more of that chapter, both backward and forward, which he freely did, and asked me, why I did require that of him? I told him, that we heard the Quakers denied the scripture, and that they would not read them. He said, there were many false reports of them. And truly when he read the scripture so readily, I concluded in myself, that what was reported of them was not true; and he saw that he had reached to the witness of God in me. Then he exhorted me to take heed to that light that shined in my heart, and did shew me my vain thoughts, and reprove me in secret for every idle word and action; saying, that "that was the true light, that lighteth every man that cometh into the world;" and in that light, I should see more light, and that would open the scriptures to me, and that I should receive a measure of the same spirit that gave them forth; and further, he told me, it was "the more sure word of prophecy, unto which I did well, if I took heed as unto a light that shineth in a dark place, until the day dawn, and the day-star arise in your hearts, 2 Peter i. 19. And he spoke much of the inward work, and the operation of God's Holy Spirit upon the soul; recommending me to the "Grace of God, that bringeth salvation, teaching us, that denying ungodliness and worldly lusts, we should live soberly, righteously and godly in the present world," Tit. ii. 11, 12. And so he departed from our house, and I set him a little along on his way.

Now when I came back from him, the consideration of his words took fast hold on me, that I could not go from under them; and the more I waited in that light that he recommended me to, the more my former peace, and that in which I formerly took comfort in, was broken; and herein I came to see, that our former building could not stand, for we built upon that which the apostle called "wood, hay, and stubble." Here I came to a loss of all my former knowledge; and my former performances proved but a sandy foundation. Then I did, with much humility and poverty of spirit, beg of Almighty God, that I might build upon that rock, that the true church of Christ was built upon, that the gates of hell might not prevail against me.

But for all this, I was yet afraid of being deceived by the Quakers; yet where to go outwardly for advice and counsel I knew not. For I saw that my former teachers were upon a sandy foundation. So I desired that the God of Abraham, Isaac, and Jacob, would be my Teacher and Instructor; for I believed that the prophecy of the prophets would be fulfilled, and that the Lord would make a new covenant with his people now, as he did promise by the mouth of the prophet Jeremiah xxxi. 31—34. "Behold, the days come, saith the Lord, that I will make a new covenant with the house of Israel, and with the house of Judah; not according to the covenant that I made with their fathers, in the day that I took them by the hand to bring them out of the land of Egypt, which my covenant they brake, although I was an husband unto them, saith the Lord: but this shall be the covenant that I will make with the house of Israel. After those days, saith the Lord, I will put my law in their inward parts, and write it in their hearts, and will be their God, and they shall be my people. And they shall teach no more every man his neighbour, and every man his brother, saying, Know ye the Lord: for they shall all know me, from the least of them unto the greatest of them, saith the Lord: for I will forgive their iniquity, and I will remember their sin no more."

These and the like precious promises I was made willing to take hold on, and waited for the fulfilling of them in myself, and of that which Christ said to the Jews, John vi. 45. "It is written in the prophets, And they shall be all taught of God. Every man therefore that hath heard, and hath learned of the Father, cometh unto me." He that cometh unto Christ Jesus the Light, that lighteth every man that cometh into the world, though their sins and their iniquities be great, they shall in no wise be cast out. And it is said, "And all thy children shall be taught of the Lord, and great shall be the peace of thy children," Isaiah liv. 13.

Richard Davies had now come to the parting of the ways. He was convinced of the reality and necessity of religion, but he was also convinced that he knew nothing yet as he ought to know, and that there was a knowledge of a more certain and satisfactory kind than that he had hitherto built his religion upon.

It had evidently come to be part of Richard Davies' belief under the influence of the teachers of the letter, that an outward baptism with water, and the outward eating and drinking of bread and wine were commanded in the scripture as acts or ceremonies to be observed by

Christians in perpetuity. He came to see, however, that they are no parts of the dispensation of which Christ Jesus is the immediate Minister; that the outward supper and the outward baptism were but figures (permitted for a time), of that which is to be inwardly known and experienced, by the washing of regeneration and the renewals of the Holy Ghost which comes with baptizing force, either accompanying the spiritual labours of those who are called, gifted, and commissioned from above, or immediately as a part of the operations of the Spirit upon the willing soul; he also saw that the supper is only truly enjoyed as the soul feeds on the living bread which comes down from heaven, and opens the door to Him who has graciously promised, " I will come in to him, and will sup with him, and he with me."

When I came to know a little of the teachings of the Lord, I took my leave of all my former formal teachers, and many times went to the woods and other by-places, where none might see me, to wait upon the Lord, where I was much broken, and tendered by the power of God. And though I did begin to see a little of myself, and something of the goodness of God, yet still I was afraid of being deceived, for I had read and heard that Satan himself is "transformed into an angel of light," 2 Cor. xi. 14. And lest this man should be as the same apostle said, in ver. 13. "For such are false apostles, deceitful workers, transforming themselves into the apostles of Christ."

I desired of the Lord that I might see this poor man once again, for I knew not where to see the face of any called a Friend; and it pleased God that he came again that way, and I desired of my master and mistress to give him lodging, and that he might be with me, to which they consented. Then I queried of him their way of worship, and concerning those two great ordinances, so called, that we so much relied upon, viz. the *Bread*, and *Wine*, and *Baptism*, and the scripture, to know what was their judgment of them; to which he gave me some satisfaction. In the morning I parted with him, and to the best of my knowledge, I saw him no more for several years after.

In all this time I still kept my retirement in the wood, or some other private place; and there in my waiting, I desired of the Lord, that I might be farther satisfied by himself, as to those things; first, whether the scriptures were the Word of God, as was said and preached unto us they were, and the way to life and salvation? Then the first chapter of John came under my serious consideration in my meditation, which said, "In the beginning was the Word, and the Word was with God, and the Word was God, the same was in the beginning with God. All things were made by him, and without him was not any thing made that was made. In him was life, and the life was the light of men; and the light shineth in darkness, and the darkness comprehended it not." I considered that the Word was in the beginning with God the Father, and that no part of the scriptures were written until Moses, who we understand, was the first writer of those scriptures we have; the apostle tells us here, that "the law was given by Moses, but grace and truth came by Jesus Christ:" in this word there was life; Paul tells us, that "the letter killeth, but the Spirit giveth life;" now this life is the light of men, and the Word was before the scriptures were written. By this we may see the word of God is Christ Jesus, that was with the Father before the world began, "without him there was not any thing made that was made." The history that Moses gives us,

C

is said to be written about 3000 years after the creation of the world, therefore the scriptures cannot properly be the Word of God.

We may see by the following remarks, that Richard Davies did not make it his business to depreciate the scriptures, but rather to come to the right use of them, and to give forth a testimony to guide others to such use. R. D. was led to see as others who witnessed a " good confession" in his age, that the scriptures are not the primary fount of religious truth, and are not entitled to a name which only belongs to the Divine Word or Light which lighteth every man that cometh into the world, and not exclusively those who are privileged with the possession of the scriptures. We see, too, that dependence on this Word was intimately connected in R. D.'s experience as to living spiritual worship, and his coming out of the will-worship which prevailed around him.

I, with many more, was under that mistake that the Jews were in, who thought they might have eternal life in the scriptures; Christ saith, John v. 39. " Search (or ye search) the scriptures, for in them ye think ye have eternal life, and they are they which testify of me; and ye will not come to me that ye might have life." As he is the life, so he is the way to the Father; " I am the way, and the truth, and the life: no man cometh unto the Father but by me," John xiv. 6. As for the scriptures, I was a great lover, and a great reader of them, and took great pleasure in searching of them, thinking that would make me wise unto salvation, as Paul said to Timothy, " And that from a child thou hast known the holy scriptures, which are able to make thee wise unto salvation, through faith, which is in Christ Jesus," 2 Tim. iii. 15. This main thing was wanting; the true and saving faith; which is, the gift of God. " It is by grace we are saved through faith, not of ourselves, it is the gift of God," Eph. ii. 8. So it is the grace of God that brings salvation, and not the bare historical knowledge of the scriptures. Too many take a great deal of pride in a literal knowledge of them; some for their gain and profit; others take pleasure in them, by wresting them to vindicate their false and erroneous opinions, that gender to strife and contention, and take little or no notice of that meek, holy, and lovely spirit of life that gave them forth, for they are of no private interpretation; " but holy men of God spake them as they were moved by the Holy Ghost," 2 Pet. i. 20, 21.

Men may have a great literal knowledge of the scriptures, and yet remain in error, because they know them not, as they ought to do, nor the power that was in the holy men that gave them forth; so I may say, as Christ said to the Jews, " You err, not knowing the scriptures, nor the power of God," Mat. xxii. 29. So that which gives the true knowledge of God, and a right understanding of the scriptures, is the power of God; and I may say with the apostle, " For God, who commanded the light to shine out of darkness, hath shined in our hearts, to give the light of the knowledge of the glory of God, in the face of Jesus Christ," 2 Cor. iv. 6. And as men and women come to mind this light, that is, the Spirit of God, and to obey it, they shall come to the comfort of the scriptures, as the same apostle says, " For whatsoever things were written aforetime, were written for our learning; that we through patience and comfort of the scriptures, might have hope," Rom. xv. 4.

And being under a serious consideration of what I read in the scripture, believing the Spirit of the Lord to be the interpreter thereof; those great mysteries that were hid from ages and generations, and are hid now in this our age from many, are come to be revealed by the Spirit of God, and if they would have comfort in reading the scriptures, they must wait in that measure of the spirit, which God hath given them, which is the only key that opens them to the understanding of those that are truly conscientious in the reading of them; and though I read them formerly, as many do now, without a true sense and a due consideration, yet now I can bless God for them, and have a great comfort in the reading of them; they being no more as a sealed book unto me, and many more, who wait for the assistance of God's holy Spirit, in their duties and performances that the Lord requires of them, for without him we know that we can do nothing that is pleasing unto him: though formerly we ran, in our own time and wills, to preach and pray, not having such a due regard to the leading and moving of the Spirit of the Lord; yet, I bless God, it is not so now. Many times, when I did arise from my knees in a formal way of prayer, a reproof was very near me, " Who required this at thy hands? It is sparks of thy own kindling." I was afraid that I should "lie down in sorrow," as was said to some by the Lord, in Isaiah l. 11.

But as to this head, I shall briefly conclude, though much more might be said to the honour of the holy scriptures; but this is my desire, that they that read them, may come to that which will give them a right understanding thereof: "For there is a spirit in man, and the inspiration of the Almighty giveth them understanding," Job xxxii. 8.

Then, as concerning water baptism, which I had under consideration, though I was no admirer of it, being not of the persuasion of re-baptizing. Those that were Independents, were not so much at first for re-baptizing; but afterward it prevailed more among them in these parts, when one Henry Jessy came here-aways. And about that time it was, that I came from among them.

We gather from the following that the customary language on the borders of Wales, even in the 17th century, involved the use of *you* to a single person; whether it was looked on as a mark of respect or otherwise, we are not clearly informed, in any case, the origin of such a confusion of speech, which now is nearly universal, was pride and corruption, and R. D. found that the cross he was called to take up forbade compliance with this custom. Ever since his time there have been those who have had to pass through a similar experience, and depart from forms of speech which tend to nourish the heathen spirit.

I had much reasoning, and various consultations in my mind concerning this, and the bread and wine. And when I was satisfied as to those weighty concerns, I thought I might rest there, and keep my old customs and fashions, and language; but that would not do, I had no peace therein: God shewed me the customs of the nation were vain, and our language not according to the language of God's people, recorded in the scriptures of truth. So I made a conscientious search into this also:—where I found the great Creator of heaven and earth, who by the word of his power made all things therein, created man in his own image, " In the image of God created he him: male and female created he them. And God blessed them, and gave them dominion over all things that he had created on the earth; and Adam gave names to them. And God took him, and put him in the garden of Eden, to dress it and to keep it. And the Lord commanded the man, saying, Of every tree of the garden *thou* mayest freely eat," Gen. ii. 15, 16. This is the first *Thou* to man, that I read of in the scripture; and the great Creator said, "Every thing that he had made was very good," Gen. i. 31. and his language to man was very good and pure. Then again, when Adam transgressed the law and commandment of God, "the Lord God called unto Adam, and said unto him, Where art *thou?* And he said, I heard thy voice in the garden, and I was afraid, because I was naked," Gen. iii. 9. 10. Here was the language of God to man, and the language of man to God. And in the searching of the scriptures, I found that all the holy men of God used that language, and Christ taught his disciples to pray in that language; "Our Father, which art in heaven, hallowed be *thy* name, *thy* kingdom come, *thy* will be done on earth as it is in heaven," Mat. vi. And withal, I knew a little grammar, and how that it was improper to say *vos* [you] to one single person, instead of *tu* [thou]. And though the learned in our nation spoke it, yet I thought Christians should not use it, but should take the Spirit of God, according to the scripture, to be their rule, and not to follow the confused language of the heathens; for the Lord, by the mouth of his prophet, commanded his people, "Learn not the way of the heathen,—for the customs of the people are vain," Jer. x. 2, 3. I also believed, that the Lord would return to his people a pure language in these days, as was promised in the days of old concerning Israel: then, when they returned to the Lord, he would bring them out of their captivity: "For then, saith the Lord, will I turn to the people a pure language, that they may all call upon the name of the Lord to serve him with one consent," Zeph. iii. 9.

Thus I was conscientiously concerned to speak the pure language of *thee* and *thou* to every one, without respect of persons, which was a great thing to me, though it seem to some but a weak and foolish thing, yet when the Lord lays the necessity of speaking the truth to all, in that language that God and all his servants used, it comes to be of a greater weight than many light, airy people think it is. The sayings of Christ came to my mind, when he said, "Whosoever will be my disciple, let him deny himself, and take up his cross daily and follow me," Luke ix. 23. He doth not say he *should do it*, but *let him do it*, imperatively; which was a command, viz. "That we should deny ourselves, and follow him:" see also Mat. xvi. 24. And moreover it is said, " He that taketh not his cross, and followeth after me, is not worthy of me," Mat. x. 38.

This necessity being laid upon me, I spoke to my master in that dialect; he was not offended at it, because he was convinced of the truth of it, and that it ought to be spoken to every one; but when I gave it to my mistress, she took a stick and gave me such a blow upon my bare head, that made it swell and sore for a considerable time; she was so disturbed at it, that she swore she would kill me, though she should be hanged for me; the enemy had so possessed her, that she was quite out of order; though beforetime she very seldom, if ever, gave me an angry word. But I considered, that the enmity was between the two seeds, and that "that which was born after the flesh, did persecute him that is born after the spirit." I being well satisfied of the truth in myself remembered Christ's words, " He that loveth father or mother more than me, is not worthy of me; and he that loveth son or daughter more than me, is not worthy of me; and he that findeth his life, shall lose it; and he that loseth his life for my sake, shall find it," Mat. x. 37, 39.

The Almighty God put it in my heart to consider the cost, and that through tribulation I was to enter the kingdom of heaven; and I was faithful in this testimony that I had to bear. I was much encouraged to go on in that strait and narrow way, that God shewed me I was to walk in. I also considered the saying of Christ, "Whosoever doth not bear his cross, and come after me, cannot be my disciple." Again, "Which of you, intending to build a tower, sitteth not down first and counteth the cost, whether he hath sufficient to finish it? Lest haply after he hath laid the foundation, and is not able to finish it, all that behold it, begin to mock him saying, This man began to build, but was not able to finish," Luke xiv. 27—30.

This consideration was weighty with me, lest I should begin to take up the cross, and to walk in this way, and should not be able to hold out to the end; first, because of the temptation of Satan, the lust of the flesh, and the sinful customs and fashions of this world, which were very prevalent; and the weight and burthen that was upon me was great, having none in the country to be an help to me in the time of my exercise, but the Lord alone, that hath promised to be with his people in all their troubles and exercises, and that he would not leave them nor forsake them. I was very ready and willing to take hold of his promises; and my prayers unto him were, *That he would enable me to go through all things that he required.* I was sensible, that without the assistance of his holy Spirit, I could not perform that service which he required of me.

At this time the Quakers were the only people or denomination, whose religious principles led them to adhere strictly to *thee* and *thou* to everyone, and to refuse the compliment of doffing the hat; there were also other matters, which caused them to become singular. It is seldom that professing Quakers follow in the steps of their predecessors, but the small Society of *Primitive Friends* still observes a good degree of plainness of speech and dress; R.D. continues,—

I was now first called a Quaker, because I said to a single person *thee* and *thou*, and kept on my hat, and did not go after the customs and fashions of the world, that other professors lived and walked in. Though some of them would complain of their formalities, and were weary of the fashions of the world; yet they did not take up their cross, and leave them.

The rage of my mistress was not yet abated, though she had nothing against me, but not conforming to the corrupt language and vain customs of the world; for I laboured to keep a conscience void of offence, both towards God and men; I did my work and service honestly and justly, " not with eye service, as men-pleasers, but in singleness of heart, as the servant of Christ, doing the will of God from the heart," Ephes. vi. 5, 6, and ver. 8. " Knowing that whatsoever good thing any man doth, the same shall he receive of the Lord, whether he be bond or free."

In thus doing, I had great comfort from the Lord, and did receive from him living satisfaction and encouragement to go on in my way; remembering that scripture that saith, " The righteous shall hold on his way, and he that hath clean hands shall be stronger and stronger," Job xvii. 9. I might also say with Job, " But he knoweth the way that I take, when he hath tried me, I shall come forth as gold; my foot hath tried his steps; his way have I kept, and not declined; neither have I gone back from the commandment of his lips: I have esteemed the words of his mouth more than my necessary food," Job xxxiii. 10—12. The Lord kept me, and his people, very meek and low in our minds, in a self-denying spirit; we waited for the living Word, that came with a living voice, from him that speaks from heaven to us by his Spirit; so that he gave us to discern between the voice of wisdom, and the voice of the strange woman, which is the voice of the flesh, and the lust thereof; and the living voice is the voice of *Christ in us the hope of glory;* which voice we esteemed more than our necessary food. For obeying this voice, we came to be mocked and derided; "and they spoke all manner of evil against us, and hated us for his name's sake," Mat. x. 22. I remembered what Christ hath told us in Luke xxi. 12. "They shall lay their hands on you, and persecute you, delivering you up to the synagogues, and into prisons, being brought before kings and rulers for my name's sake: and it shall return to you for a testimony. Settle it therefore in your hearts, not to meditate before what ye shall answer; for I will give you a mouth and wisdom, which all your adversaries shall not be able to gainsay or resist," Luke xxi. 13—15.

These and the like afflictions I was to meet with, if I truly and faithfully followed the Lord Jesus Christ; therefore I laboured to put on the whole armour of light, that I might be able to withstand the fiery darts of the wicked one, who sought to weaken my faith, and to persuade me of the hardness, straightness, and narrowness of the way, that I should not be able to hold out to the end, seeing there was not any in this country to help and assist me; but the fiery darts of the enemy that I felt, came more by his servants than otherwise. Very prevalent he was in this poor misled woman, my mistress, who was persuaded by him to kill me, and shed innocent blood; and one time, when she thought it a fit opportunity to execute her will and cruelty, she fell into a great rage, and I was freely given up to die that hour by her; but the Lord was pleased to accept of my freewill offering, and I may say with the apostle, "that I accounted not my life dear to myself, that I might finish my course with joy." And the Lord alone appeared to my deliverance, and made her more moderate the rest of my servitude, it being somewhat less than two years; and after I went away, the Lord visited her with a sharp fit of sickness, in which time she spoke to her husband and them that were with her, that she thought she should not die till she had asked me forgiveness, and desired them to send for me if it were London; and so they did: I could freely forgive her, for that I had done long since, and I prayed to my heavenly Father that he might forgive her also. I sent to her, and it pleased God to touch her with a sense of his love, and lengthened her days, she confessing oftentimes the wrong she had done to an honest, careful young man, as she said I had been, who minded her husband's inward and outward good, more than they did themselves. It pleased God to order it so, that she had a visit from me, before she went out of this world, and very comfortable and acceptable it was to her; and in a little time she ended her days in peace, and was buried in friends' burying-place near Dolgelly in Merionethshire.

About this time, 1657, it was the great talk of the country that I was become a Quaker. My parents were much concerned about me. I was informed that the priest of Welch-pool, W. Longford, went to them and told them, that I was gone distracted, and that they should see for some learned men to come to me and restore me to my senses. I had not been yet with my father nor mother, but waited for freeness and clearness in myself, and then I went to see them, and in my way I visited an old friend of mine, a professor, and had a little opportunity to speak to him of the things of God, and his goodness to me, and a young man, called David Davies, was then convinced of the truth: this was on a seventh-day, in the afternoon: and when I was clear there, I went to Welch-pool to my parents. It was a trouble to them, to see that I did not, as formerly, go down upon my knees to ask their blessing, and bow to them, and take off my hat. My father soon turned his back upon me. I had heard of his displeasure, and that he had said, he would leave me nothing; saying to my relations, that they thought to have had comfort of me, but now they expected none, but that I would go up and down the country, crying Repent! Repent! Now if my father should have cast me off upon such an account, I was well persuaded it was for Christ's and the gospel's sake. I remembered David's condition, when he said, "Hide not thy face far from me, put not thy servant away in anger: thou hast been my help, leave me not, neither forsake me, O God of my salvation; when my father and my mother forsake me, then the Lord will take me up: teach me thy way, O Lord, and lead me in a plain path because of mine enemies," Psalm xxvii. 9—11.

At length my mother came tenderly to me, and took a view of me, looking on my face, and she saw that I was her child, and that I was not, as they said, bewitched, or transformed into some other likeness; which was reported of Quakers then, and that they bewitched people to their religion, &c. Thus they deceived them and many others, with strange stories, and we were accounted with the apostles, deceivers, yet true. And when I discoursed with her out of the scriptures, her heart was much tendered and affected with the goodness of God towards me; she went to see for my father, and when she found him, said unto him, "Be of good comfort, our son is not as was reported of him, we hope to have comfort of him yet."

The next paragraph records an incident of a character

not very uncommon in those days. The term *church* was denied by R. D. and his brethren to a building of mortar and stone,—it expressed more than the truth, and tended to foster a spirit of superstitious reverence amongst the people for places supposed to be holier than others.

These buildings the Friends called " steeple-houses," being at that time, as now, national property, and the national will no longer expressing itself by the use of Episcopal forms, the Book of Common Prayer was banished from them, and persons of Presbyterian, Independent, or Baptist tenets usually officiated there; it then sometimes happened that those who had been brought to the dispensation of the Spirit—the despised Quakers, felt themselves commissioned to be present and offer a Divine message or testimony to the congregation, which tended to spread a knowledge of the Truth.

But when my father came to his house, he spoke not much to me that night. The next day, being the first day of the week, when I heard the bells ring, it came upon me to go to the steeple-house, to visit that priest that had told my father, I was gone distracted, &c., and when he was at his worship, I went to our own seat to my father; (there was no common-prayer read then to the people, as part of their worship in those days) there I sat still till he had done, and when he had done what he had then to say, I stood up and told him, That he might do well to stay, and make good the false doctrine, that day, if he could; and if I was distracted, as he reported, that he might labour to restore me to my right senses again. But I spoke but a little while, ere I was taken away to prison, with the young man before mentioned, that came to see for me, and found me in the steeple-house, so both of us were taken; there we were prisoners that night, in which time many far and near came to see us, expecting that we were some deformed creatures. God gave me a seasonable exhortation to them to fear the Lord, and indeed to cry, "Repent, repent, for the kingdom of heaven was at hand;" letting them know, "that we were God's workmanship, created anew in Christ Jesus;" with much more to that effect. I spoke to them from the scripture, which was much to their satisfaction, and we praised God, that kept us in his fear and counsel.

We were committed to prison on that law, made in Oliver's days, that none were to speak to the priest or preachers, neither at their worship, nor coming and going. The next morning we were had before the chief magistrate of the town of Welch-pool, and after some discourse with him, it seemed good to him to discharge us, for he could find nothing justly to accuse us of, except concerning the law of our God.

So we went to our homes, the young man to his father's, and I to my master's; he suffered much violence by his father, in regard that he could not conform himself to that dry, dead, and formal praying that his father used; his father rose from off his knees when he was at prayer, and took a staff, and did violently beat his son, and against natural affection, he took a lock and chain, and chained him out of doors in a cold frosty night. Thus our sufferings began to increase, for the testimony of our consciences towards God; but blessed be the name of the Lord, who preserved his people that trusted in him, saith my soul.

CHAPTER III.

**PIERCING POWER IN A SILENT MEETING AT SHREWS-
BURY—VISIT TO A GAY COMPANY OF DANCERS—ROGER
PRICHARD—VAVASOR POWELL—MEETINGS IN THE
OPEN-AIR DECIDED ON—GOES TO LONDON—INWARD
POINTINGS TOWARD MARRIAGE—MEETS GEORGE FOX—
IMPRISONED AT MONTGOMERY AND AT SHREWSBURY,
BRIDGENORTH.**

A little after this I came to hear, that some of the people that were called Quakers, were at Shrewsbury in the county of Salop, being distant from the place of my abode about eighteen miles; I waited for an opportunity to go to see them, and the way of their worship, for as yet I had not seen any of them, but that one poor man before mentioned. When the time called Christmas came, my master's work being somewhat over for a while, I got leave to go so far. I went first to the house of John Millington, where many friends resorted, and they of the town came to see me in great love and tenderness, and much brokenness of heart was among us, though but few words. We waited to feel the Lord among us, in all our comings together. When the First day of the week came, we went to a meeting at W. Pane's, at the Whyte Cop, where we had a silent meeting, and though it was silent from words, yet the word of the Lord was among us, it was a hammer and a fire, it was sharper than any two-edged sword, it pierced through our inward parts, it melted and brought us into tears, that there was scarcely a dry eye among us; the Lord's blessed power overshadowed our meeting, and I could have said, that God alone was master of that assembly. The next day as I was preparing homewards, having had a considerable time with friends there, and being much comforted with the goodness of God, and unfeigned love of the brethren, we heard that John ap John was come to town, and was to have a meeting there; I staid that meeting, where I heard the first friend that was called a Quaker, preach in a meeting, and when I heard him, I thought he spoke as one having authority, and not as the Scribes, his words were so sound and piercing.

After this meeting at Shrewsbury, I came home to my master's house, where I was under many considerations, and especially that of Christ's words, "Ye are the light of the world. A city that is set on a hill cannot be hid. Neither do men light a candle, and put it under a bushel, but on a candlestick, and it giveth light unto all that are in the house. Let your light so shine before men, that they may see your works, and glorify your Father which is in heaven," Mat. v. 14—16.

I was sensible that God had opened my understanding, and lighted my candle, and given me a sense and feeling of my own state and condition, how that I had been in darkness, and under the region and shadow of death; and God having shewed mercy and kindness unto me, in calling of me from this great darkness to the marvellous light of his dear Son Christ Jesus, that is, "the light of the world, that enlighteneth every man that cometh into the world;" I was made willing not to hide my candle, as it were under a bushel, or to hide my talent in the earth; but in the love of God, I was made willing to let that light, which he pleased by his grace to enlighten me withal, shine before men, that they might come. "to glorify their heavenly father, which is in heaven," Mat. v. 16.

The next public service that the Lord required of me, was to go and give my testimony for him, and to warn a company of people to think of their latter end, who were met to dance and to play, at what they called a merry night,‡ not far from my master's house. When I came within the room where they were dancing, the fiddler ceased playing, and they dancing; I declared the word of the Lord among them. That which was chiefly before me was that of Job; "They send forth their little ones like a flock, and their children dance. They take the timbrel and harp, and rejoice at the sound of the organ. They spend their days in mirth, and in a moment go down to the grave," Job xxi. 11—13. When I had discharged myself of what lay upon me, I parted in love and peace from them, and they thanked me for my good exhortation, and some of them came to set me home.

About this time, 1658, I heard of one that was called a Quaker, who was come from Ireland to Llanfyllin,* a town in the county of Montgomery, and in the love of God I went upon the first day of the week to visit him; where we had a comfortable refreshing meeting together, and the Lord's presence was with us, though we were strangers one to another, as to the outward, yet we had fellowship and unity one with another in the inward life of righteousness; his name was Roger Prichard.† He tarried not long there, but went back again to Ireland;

---

* Spelt Llanvilling in the English edition.

‡ Noswaith lawen

† It is not improbable that R. P., an ancestor of the Editor's, was a Welsh-speaking man who had either served in the Army in Ireland, or had gone there for trading purposes not long before. His convincement, too, must have been recent, as Truth was not promulgated in that country before 1653. A stranger to Wales would hardly have had a concern to live at Llanfyllin.

though it was said, he came to these parts with an intention to stay here, and to bear his testimony for God in this dark corner of North Wales; but he not being faithful to God, who sent him here, as he was going back he suffered great losses by sea, and lost his good condition also, and turned back to the vanities of the world, which was a great sorrow and exercise to me: but the Lord visited him again, as may be seen hereafter. Thus I was left alone again.

I continued, as the Lord made way for me, to visit those in whom I found any inclination to the things that were good, and there was one William Davies convinced of the truth with me. I was also made willing to visit the Independent meeting, and those people that I formerly belonged to, that were a separate people, * gathered together chiefly by Vavasor Powell, before mentioned, a zealous man in his day. But when truth broke forth in this country, I being the first to receive it in these parts, did separate myself from them, in love to that blessed truth that I received, and it became my true teacher. So Vavasor Powell proved angry [like many more of the teachers of that day who saw their flocks diminishing], and preached much against the Quakers, their way and principles; I hearing this, came to a place called Cloddiaucochion, near Welch-pool, to the meeting, expecting to find him there; but he was not there. John Griffithes, a justice of the peace in those days, was preaching there. When I came in among them, they seemed uneasy; and when I had an opportunity, I bore a testimony for God, and his son Christ Jesus, his way, truth, and people, which they preached against. When I had done what I had to say, he went on again; and when I found something more

---

* " A separate people " means " Independents."

upon my spirit to declare among them, this John Griffithes commanded to take me away; and a near relation of mine, that owned the house, took me in his arms, and led me out of the house through the fold, and through a gate that opened to the common, and shut the gate after me. There I sat under an ash tree, weeping and mourning to see the blindness, darkness, and hardness of heart, pride, and haughtiness, that were come over a people who once were loving, kind, and humble in spirit. As I sat weightily under a serious consideration, what and when would be the end of these formalities and hardness of heart, I prayed to the Lord for them. And the word of the Lord came to me, that though they put me out of their house, yet in time they would own truth, and that house should be a meeting-place for friends. Of this a further account may be seen hereafter. So I went away, well satisfied of the love and goodness of God to me that day, in giving me comfort and consolation, for my tears of sorrow and affliction, that I met with a little before; and I remembered the saying of the apostle, Heb. xii. 11. "Now no chastening for the present seemeth to be joyous, but grievous; nevertheless, afterward it yieldeth the peaceable fruit of righteousness, unto them that are exercised thereby."

After this, I still waited to know the will and counsel of God, and that he might direct me in my way and order my steps in this spiritual travail; for I had none to look unto, but to him alone, who was all-sufficient to carry on the work which he had begun, though often by weak, poor, mean, and contemptible instruments in the eyes of the world. Well might I say with the apostle, "But God hath chosen the foolish things of the world, to confound the wise; and God hath chosen the weak things of the world to confound the things which are mighty; and base things of the world, and things which are despised, hath God chosen, yea, and things which are not, to bring to nought things that are," 1 Cor. i. 27, 28.

About this time I went to visit some young men, my former companions in profession of religion; two or three of them were convinced, and received the truth. When we were come to the number of four, it was with me, that we ought to meet together in the name of the Lord; for I remembered the promise of Christ, who said, "Where two or three are gathered together in my name, there am 1 in the midst of them," Mat. xviii. 20.

So we all agreed to meet together, but none of us had a house of his own to meet in. We determined therefore to meet upon a hill in a common as near as we could, for the convenience of each other, we living some miles distant one from another. There we met in silence, to the wonder of the country. When the rain and weather beat upon one side of the hill, we went to the other side. We were not free to go into any neighbour's enclosures, for they were so blind, dark, and ignorant, that they looked upon us as witches, and would go away from us, some crossing† themselves with their hands about their foreheads and faces.

Richard Davies tells us here that some of his religious acquaintances were "convinced" and "received the Truth." Now the reader may be at a loss to understand the meaning of such expressions; they are not indeed fully clear without actual personal experience of such convincement. We may, however, refer back to R. D.'s previous life and way of worship, and comparing that with his account of

---

* The reader should remember that only 100 years before Roman Catholicism was the religion of the Country; and in remote parts of Wales, some of the old superstitious practices survived long after Richard Davies's time.

the meetings spoken of below, notice a great change in his manner of worship which was a consequence of his "convincement."

When R.D. frequented the Independent Meetings he and his friends were used to pray in their own will and time, and there is every reason to believe that preaching, praying, and singing took up the whole time professedly devoted to Divine worship, yet, a worship in reality of which the spirit of man rather than the Spirit of God was the leader; R.D. himself states that he was at a loss, and knew not which way to take, in order to have peace and comfort in his performances. Now compare such meetings, with that held at Shrewsbury, where not a word was spoken, but in which those present came under the ministry of the living Word which is as a hammer and a fire, and in consequence there was scarce a dry eye among them.

So these young men whose minds had been so far enlightened, as to see that all good was of God, came together to worship in public and in the open air. What an opportunity it would appear for enlightened minds to preach the Truth to their neighbours, to inform them of what was faulty in their worship, and of what doctrines they were called on to support. But no, they had, it is true, to preach a powerful sermon to the whole country side, but it was a sermon without words. The Episcopalians who were then ousted from the old parish mass-houses,(commonly called churches), could not perform their public worship without a book, nor without the presence of a man supposed to be qualified in some mysterious way by the laying on of hands, to minister spiritual things. The dominant sects of that time represented at Welshpool by Vavasor Powell, gathered people by continued vocal exercises, and without these, their meetings could not be held; but here were these few young men neither preaching nor praying vocally, but meeting for public worship to the " wonder of the Country."

If it be asked why not preach, we might well query in return, why preach without an immediate command, why not wait in silence ?

For this, there are several reasons, all centreing in the relations which the creature bears toward the Creator.

1.—God is a Spirit.
2.—The spirit of man needs to be ministered to by the Spirit of God.
3.— Mere words at best only give notions of Truth, and cannot effect this ministry, *i.e.*, they cannot feed the soul with heavenly bread, but only keep the mind in activity.
4.— Everything in worship not inspired by the Spirit of God, is a hindrance rather than a help. Therefore words without a call and Divine leading are to be abstained from.

A meeting in the *name* of Christ, that is in his power, may then be a wholly silent meeting outwardly, yet one in which the work of the new creation goes forward, and the soul receives sustenance and strength, or if any words be spoken they will be in " demonstration of the Spirit, and with power." R.D. goes on to say :—

Thus we continued for some time, till two of them left me; one of them was put apprentice by friends to William Shewen,† of London. The other young man was a soldier in Oliver Cromwell's days, and he got, as soon as he could, to be disbanded, so he went to Gloucestershire, and lived among friends. The third was one William Davies, that lived hard by me, and we met together for some time; but one time he staid longer than usual, and a foul dark spirit possessed him, so that the little time we were together, was not comfortable to me, and when we had broke up the meeting, by way of discourse, he asked me, how I did think we should stand in the face of the whole country. I answered him with great zeal, the Serpent, the Serpent, the same that beguiled the woman in Paradise, hath beguiled thee, thou wilt not be able to stand. And while we were yet discoursing, I saw my master coming, who was also convinced, but was not faithful to that good Spirit that convinced him of the truth, and shewed him what he ought to do, but did it not, yet he continued loving to friends, and frequented their meetings to his latter end. As I looked back, I saw him coming towards us, with two women following him, the one was his wife, my cruel mistress, the other was his sister; they both had staves in their hands, and when they came unto us, the sister began to beat her brother my master, and my mistress set a beating of W. Davies. So his trial came very quickly, and W. Davies came no more to meet with me,

---

† William Shewen, was a draper of the City of London, . . who is best known to posterity by his Meditations and Experiences, which has been successively re-printed, the last edition at Newport in 1893, and it is nearly out of print. This valued work has little to say on the historical parts of Christianity which are acknowledged by most professors, nor in what might be called Christian theory and abstract doctrine. It contains a clear testimony to the nature and effects of spiritual religion as realized inwardly in actual experience.

nor any other friends, for many years; yet he afterwards came among friends, and continued with them to the end of his days, and was buried among them. It so happened that I had never a blow among them, and if I had received any, I had learned of Christ Jesus, my Lord and master, to suffer patiently for his name's sake, and not to depart from him, though my trials, temptations, and afflictions were not a few; so that I may say with the apostle, "But none of these things move me, neither count I my life dear unto myself, so that I might finish my course with joy." Acts xx. 24. 2 Cor. iv. 17. Mat. x. 37, 38, 39.

These young men going away thus, I was left alone again, but still I kept waiting upon the Lord, to know his will and good pleasure concerning me; and when the time of my apprenticeship was over, I found freedom to go to London, to visit friends there, which was in the year 1658-9; and finding many good and living * friends there, I settled to my trade, being a felt maker, and very well satisfied I was, that I could go to meetings, and follow my business. When any thing would come to my mind of this my native country, barren and uninhabited with friends and truth, I endeavoured to shut it out, and to keep where I was, and I did what I could; but all my fair pretences and reasonings would not do, disobedient to the Lord I was, and trouble and sorrow, and judgment from the Lord came upon me, for not obeying his command, to go to my own country to stand a witness for him there. In this my disobedience, I continued till I lost his presence, and he smote me with trouble within, and pain in my bones, that I could not work nor labour. In this time, friends of London were very kind and careful of me, and would freely have administered unto me, but

---

* Living in the Divine Life, with spiritual senses exercised therein

I was not willing to accept of any thing from them, so long as I had of my own. My pain of body and spirit increased upon me, till at last I was forced to bow to the will of the great God, who was too strong for me; and reasoning with him one night, upon the bed of my sorrows, he shewed me clearly, that I was to go to my own country; and I was made willing to give up to go, if he would be pleased to let me know his will and pleasure by this sign and token, that he would remove my pain. I also reasoned with him thus; that I was alone, like a pelican in the wilderness, or a sparrow on a house top. The Lord still commanded me to go, shewing that he would provide a help-meet for me. And when I had made a covenant with the Lord to go, immediately my pain was removed, and I had peace and quietness of mind and spirit. I arose next morning, and went to my work; and when those tender friends, that had a regard for me in my sickness, came to see me that morning, I was gone to work; which was to their admiration.

So the Lord gave me a little time, and he alone provided an help-meet for me; for I prayed unto him, that she might be of his own providing, for it was not yet manifest to me where she was, or who she was. But one time as I was at Horselydown meeting in Southwark, I heard a woman friend open her mouth, by way of testimony against an evil ranting spirit that did oppose friends much in those days. It came to me from the Lord that that woman was to be my wife, and to go with me to the country, and to be an help-meet for me. After meeting, I drew somewhat near to her, but spoke nothing, nor took any acquaintance with her, nor did I know when, or where I should see her again. I was very willing to let the Lord order it as it seemed best to himself, and therein I was easy; and in time the Lord brought us acquainted one with another, and she confessed that she had some sight of the same thing that I had seen concerning her. So after some time we parted, and I was freely resigned to the will of God; and when we came together again, I told her, if the Lord did order her to be my wife, she must come with me to a strange country, where there were no friends but what God in time might call and gather to himself. Upon a little consideration, she said, if the Lord should order it so, she must go with her husband, though it were to the wilderness; and being somewhat sensible of the workings of God upon her spirit in this matter, she was willing to condescend in her mind to what He wrought in her: but by hearkening to one who had not well weighed the matter, she became disobedient to what God had revealed to her; which brought great sorrow and trouble upon her. I went to see her in this poor condition, and I rested satisfied with the will of God in this concern, being freely resigned, if the Lord had wrought the same thing in her, as was in me, to receive her as his gift to me; and after some time, we waiting upon the Lord together, she arose, and declared before me, and the other friend who had begot doubts and reasonings in her mind, that in the name and power of God she consented to be my wife, and to go along with me, whither the Lord should order us; and I said, in the fear of the Lord I receive thee as the gift of God to me. So I rested satisfied in the will of God, for a further accomplishment of it.

The cross pressed upon faithful friends in many ways, and they were not exempt in the important matter of marriage; no way had been made for the effective legalization of Friends' marriages at their own meetings, and marriage by a priest amounted to an endorsement of priestly authority which would have directly contradicted the testimony given them by their Lord and Master.

Under a weighty consideration, which way to take each other in marriage, we concluded to lay our proceedings before our elders, and especially our ancient friend George Fox; (people in those days were married by a priest, or before a justice) and I told G. Fox, we thought to take each other in a public meeting; so he desired the Lord to be with us. And when we saw our clearness in the Lord, we went to the Snail meeting in Tower Street, London, in the morning; and in the afternoon to Horselydown, Southwark; and in that meeting, being the 26th of the fourth month, 1659, in the presence of God, and that assembly, we took each other to be man and wife.

God alone knew our innocency and integrity in going together. It was not for gold nor silver, nor for any outward thing; but to be serviceable to him in our age and generation, and to stand witnesses for him and his blessed truth, where he should send us. I might say with Tobias, "Thou madest Adam, and gavest him Eve his wife, for a helper and a stay; of them came mankind. Thou hast said, it is not good that man should be alone, let us make him an aid like himself." Tobit viii. 6.

Soon after, in the Lord's time, we made what haste we could to come to the country, where we believed the Lord would have us to be, and we said, O Lord, if thou wilt go with us in our way, and give us bread to eat, and raiment to put on, then, O Lord, thou shalt be our God; and the Lord was with us in all our journey, and gave unto us his sweet and comfortable presence.

Richard Davies' history now brings us to the downfall

of the old Puritan party and the rise of the Royalists, who were made tools of, as their successors are now, by ecclesiastics professedly acting in the interests of religion, to aid them in the vain attempt to crush out or repress dissent.

R. D. we see, boldly kept his hat in the presence of these Royalist justices. He and his friends had been instructed that this taking off the hat to mortal man was an honour which God would lay in the dust, and they were required to abstain from the general practice.

Soon after we came to Welch-Pool, those professors, who had been and were in great power, began to be faint-hearted, because of the report of bringing in king Charles the Second; which in a little time was accomplished, and those that were in great pomp, were brought to prison themselves. And I was had before the first justices that were made in these parts by the authority of king Charles the Second, in the year 1660, notwithstanding I was a prisoner to the magistrate of the town. When I went up before them, many of the people of the town followed me, to see what would become of me, and to what prison they would send me, or what punishment they would inflict upon me. But the Lord was with me, and I feared not man, whose breath is in his nostrils, but the living God whom I desired to obey in all things. When I was come into the room, it being in the night, colonel Mostyn, and the justices stood as people in a maze, to see me come with my hat on my head amongst them, and spoke not one word to me for some time. In a little while, I asked them, whether they sent for me there; they said, they did. One of the justices asked me, where I had that new way, and strange religion; I answered him, It was the good old way that the prophets and servants of God lived and walked in; and that way I had found, and desired to walk in it all my days. That justice was peevish, and said, I think the man is mad: I think we must have him whipped; though I answered them according to scripture, yet they were ignorant of it. They demanded of me to take the oath of allegiance and supremacy; I told them, that my Lord and Master Christ Jesus and his apostle James commanded me not to swear at all. They had a priest with them, who took upon him to question me. The first thing he asked me was, which was first, reason or scripture; I told him, reason was before scripture; God made man a reasonable creature in his own image: and the first part of the scriptures now extant, was written by Moses: the apostle tells us, "that the law came by Moses, but grace and truth came by Jesus Christ." I farther told them, "that holy men of God gave them forth as they were moved by the Holy Ghost." As to this, they seemed to be satisfied. But the priest put some ensnaring questions to me; and when I perceived it, I asked the justices what that man was; whether he was a justice of the peace or not; and, whether he was not a priest; they said, They looked upon him to be a fitter man than themselves to discourse with me about religion. I told them, I thought he was as the high-priest among the Jews, who put ensnaring questions to Christ, when he was brought before them, to seek to make him an offender; and turned myself to the justices, and desired them to take notice of that man, who laid those ensnaring questions, to seek to make me an offender. Then the priest left me, and the justices asked me, seeing I would not take the oaths, whether I would give bail; and said they would take my father's bail for my good behaviour. I told them, my cause was just, and I was innocent, and would give them no bail, for truth binds me to my good behaviour.

Then the high-sheriff, a very fair man, told me, I was a strange man, and of a strange persuasion, to come with my hat upon my head among them, and would not take the oaths nor give bail. You know said he, that Paul said to Festus, Noble Festus. I told him, that Paul had tried Festus, but I had not as yet tried him; and it might be, that I might speak of him, Noble Sheriff. Upon this they were most of them very pleasant. He asked me, whom I did know there; there were several justices my relations present, who very well knew me, but I made mention of none of them; but told them I knew the chief magistrate of the town, Charles Jones, whose prisoner I was. Then they called for him, and asked him, whether he knew me; he said, he did very well, for I was born and bred in the town among them, and was a very honest young man all along; but, said he, what devil he hath now, I know not. They asked him, whether I was his prisoner; he said, I was. Then said the justices take him again to your custody. As I was going out of the room, I told them, that I brought a good hat on my head there, but was going away without it, for some of the baser sort had conveyed it away, but the justices made diligent search about it; so it was brought me again, and put upon my head, and they parted with me very friendly, and the town magistrate took me a little from them, and bid me go home to my wife and family. Many of the inhabitants of the town accompanied me home, praising God in their way for my deliverance, for several things were threatened against me; but, blessed be God, truth was over all and had dominion; and the witness of God was reached in many of them, and the high-sheriff continued loving and kind to friends, and ready to serve them in what he could all his life-time, as also was his deputy-sheriff, and several other of the justices.

About the third month, 1660, many of those professors, captains, lieutenants, and soldiers, that were in arms in Oliver's and Richard Cromwell's days, were put in prison in the town of Montgomery. My wife and I did foresee, that I should be sent there to them, though I never was a soldier, nor bore any arms for either side. And in a little time there came a troop of horse for me, to bring me to prison. My relations offered to give bail for me, but it was not accepted. So I went to acquaint my wife of it, and to make myself ready to go with them. One of the soldiers came up stairs after me with a pistol and naked sword, and my wife raising herself up, and sitting in bed, being delivered but three days before of her first child, she said, dear husband be faithful to God, whatever becomes of me. The soldier seeing her, retreated back. So I went down to the troop of horse standing in the street before my house. There was among them one bad man, that run away in my father's debt, threatened to compel me to follow his horse's heels on foot many miles. But by this time several of the aldermen, and others of the town, were gathered together in the street, who desired this man, and others of the troop, to let me alone for that time, and they would engage body for body, that I should be in prison next morning; but they could not prevail. At length some of the aldermen fell into a rage, and bid them meddle with me if they durst; and bid me go to my house, which I was not willing to do, for great fear came upon me, lest there should be a quarrel among them concerning my going or staying. But one or two of the aldermen, being more considerate than the rest, desired their patience till the captain might be spoken with, who was then in town. He soon granted that I should stay at home that night, and be in Montgomery prison next morning, and was angry at that bad man for his incivility towards the aldermen who interceded for me; for the captain knew I was a peaceable man, and never concerned myself in fighting for one side or other. When the troop had their orders, they went on their way; and I praised God, in the multitude of his mercies, that there was no blood shed that day; for many of the young men of the town, with the aldermen, were gathered together with clubs and staves, saying, what, should a town's born child be so abused by such a bad fellow as that was, before-mentioned; my heart often trembled within me, lest anything should fall amiss in this tumult; and I desired them often, before they went to the captain, that I might go along with them towards my prison.

So that night I staid at home, and next morning took my journey towards my prison at Montgomery. I avoided the house of my uncle, a justice of the peace in this county, near my way, and brother-in-law to this captain, lest he should stop me from going to prison. So I went there myself alone, and told the marshall, John Mason, that I was come a prisoner; and he took me up to an upper garret for my lodging, but I had the liberty of the house, as well as other prisoners, there being many Presbyterians, Independents, and Baptists, who were formerly my great acquaintance; but now they appeared very strange, and would not discourse with me. I considered the reason, and was informed, that these old formal church-members or professors had agreed among themselves that they would not discourse with me, nor receive any books from me, lest the most serious inward Christians amongst them should turn Quakers. But in a little time their orders and covenants were broken, and I was moved to go to their meeting, sometimes having little to say among them, but a sigh or a groan, and a travail in my spirit for them, which did often put them out of order in their preaching and praying; and as the Lord would order it, I spoke a few words among them. A Baptist was convinced there, and came to meet with me in my room. Cadwallader Edwards was also convinced, and came up with us to meet in the prison; and then discoursings and disputes began between them and me. I wrote a few lines to send home to my wife, but knew not by whom to send it, for it was very hard to send any papers out of prison; the marshal, or jailor, would examine and search such as came in, or went out for letters. An old friend, an acquaintance of mine, came to visit her friends and brethren the professors in prison, whom I desired to carry that letter to my wife, as she went through our town of Welch-pool, to her home; she was afraid to meddle with it, partly for fear of the jailer, and also lest she should offend her brethren there. I desired her not to be afraid, for I would read it to her first, and the jailer might see it if he pleased: and after I had read it to her, she was tenderly affected, turned to her brethren again, and said, surely these people will never come to us, but we must go to them. Some time after, through much trouble and affliction, she came to receive the truth, to live in it, and obey it; her name was Margaret Bowen, wife of John Bowen, of Collfryn, and mother to Peter Bowen, in Martin's-le-Grand, London.

In a little time my service was over among those professors in that prison, and the Lord made way for my enlargement. In about two weeks I came away, and left the rest of the prisoners there, where they continued a considerable time. I was well satisfied with the goodness of God, that I found his presence, life, and power with me; a present help in the time of need, which kept me low and humble, that I durst not rejoice that spirits were made subject; but rather rejoice that I found my name written in heaven. I came home in great love and peace to my wife and family, and many of my loving neighbours rejoiced to see me.

I continued about my calling and business, and waited upon God to know his mind and will concerning me. In this time I heard of an honest old woman, who had received the truth some time before at Montgomery, her name was Ann Hamon, wife of Thomas Hamon; my wife and I went to visit her.

In the following paragraph we have a glimpse of prison discipline in the 17th century. Jailors appears to have been responsible for little beyond the due appearance of their prisoners, and often had the opportunity of making money out of them in various ways. It not unfrequently happened that Friends were very cruelly used out of mere malice, in addition to the unsuitable quarters which were the rule rather than the exception, in the case of such as did not, or could not pay for better accommodation. Indeed it was sometimes the case that even payment did not suffice to procure surroundings consistent with the ordinary conditions of health.

In the present case, R.D. and his friends insisted on their right to free lodgings and had to suffer in consequence.

About the year 1661, I went to a meeting at Edgemont near Wem, in Shropshire. Here our friend William Gibson and I were taken prisoners, with about 25 or 26 more, and sent to Shrewsbury. We found the temper of of the jailer very cruel. He threatened us with a great deal of hardship, if we did not eat of his meat, drink of his drink, and lie on his beds, and give him what he demanded. We told him, we were the king's prisoners, and demanded a free prison, and straw to lie upon; but he in a rage denied us that, and put us in a little room where there was scarce place for us to lie down. When night came, sleep came upon us, we being weary by travelling so many miles on foot, but we were made willing and able to suffer all things; so that night, we lay upon the boards, and it was pleasant unto us, being warm weather, and about the time of hay-harvest The next morning we were very fresh and well, praising God for his mercies and goodness to us, when the jailer came to us, and asked, How we liked our lodging, and how we slept: we told him, we slept in peace of conscience and quietness of mind, for we suffered for conscience-sake towards God, and durst not break the command of Christ and the apostle, who commanded us not to swear at all. For our supposed transgression was not only for meeting together, but for refusing the oaths of allegiance and supremacy.* The jailer being a very passionate, inconsiderate man, would go out in the morning from his own house, and not come back till night and then return so drunken, that he could hardly speak or stand. The next night when we went to lie down the room was so little we could not all lie down at once. The next morning we complained to the jailer, that there was not enough room for us all to lie down, and desired him to let us have a little straw, but it would not be granted us. By this time the friends of the town had

---

* The law for administering the oath of Supremacy was made soon after the accession of Queen Elizabeth, and was intended to guard against the recognition of Papal authority. After the discovery of the Gunpowder Plot, in the reign of James I., another act was made enjoining the taking of an oath of allegiance, which contained a promise to defend the throne against all conspiracies. Besse in his "Sufferings of the Quakers" says:—The edge of these old laws was now turned upon the Quakers, while the Papists, against whom they were originally made, were little molested. (Vol. I.)

liberty to come to visit us, and to bring us in some provisions; and when the door was opened for us to go into another room, there being a bedstead with cords in that room, William Gibson and I lay upon the cords, and next morning we found, that the print of the cords was not only in our clothes, but in our skin also, so that it had been easier for us to have lain upon the boards, as we did before. By this time having well observed the jailer's humour and temper, I began to be uneasy in myself to let him alone; so I watched him in the morning upon his first rising, when he came to the court before our prison door, and began to discourse with him about the prisoners that lay in such hardship. I told him, they were honest men and most of them masters of families, and had good beds to lie upon at home, but now they were content for Christ's and the Gospel's sake, to suffer that hardship, I desired him to let them have liberty to go to their friends in town at night, and to come there in the morning; and if he would not be pleased to grant them a little straw, then to let them go lie in their own beds; which he surlily denied, calling them a company of rogues and knaves, and such like terms. He asked me, What made me plead for them; I told him they were my friends. He answered, why your friends? You are no Quaker, are you? I said, I am called a Quaker. He answered, you do not look like a Quaker; and he looked me in my face and on my hands and body. I desired him not to disgrace me so, as to tell me I was no Quaker. Then he asked me, where I lived; I told him, when I was at home, I lived at Welch-pool, and my family was there. But said he, where are you now? I asked him, whether he did not know I was a prisoner there with my friends; and he asked me, whether I did lie upon the boards with them; I told him I did. He said, he was sorry for it; but went away in anger, being much discontented in himself. I did not see him till next morning, at which time I went to him again, and friendly discoursed with him; he said, he inquired about me in town, and I might take the liberty of the town. I acknowledged his kindness; but told him, it would be no comfort to me, to have the liberty of the town, and leave my friends and brethren there. He said, then I might stay there with them. So I did not see him till the next morning, then I went to him again. He was so cross and ill-conditioned, he would not suffer any other friend to speak to him. William Gibson did so judge him for his wickedness, that he kept him close in a room by himself. After five or six nights lying on the boards, I prevailed with him, that friends might have the liberty of the town in the night, and be there in the morning. So the next day he began to be more friendly to us. After some days, I desired our friend John Millington to come with me to the jailer's house, to see whether we could have leave to go home till the next assizes; but then it was not granted; but he told me, if I pleased I might go till then. I told him, he might as freely let them go as me, for most of them lived in the county, and I lived out of the county; but no more could we have that time of him. I was uneasy in myself (seeing I had got a place in him) to let him alone, and pressed for my friends' farther liberty. A little time afterwards, by serious arguments, as it was harvest time, and hard for their wives, or some of their families, to come with weekly necessaries for them, I, with my friend John Millington, prevailed with him to let them go, and he took our words for our appearance at the next assizes.

Through the goodness of God, we all returned together to Shrewsbury, to our prison, before the assizes, and found a great alteration in the jailor; he was very low and mournful. He had lost a prisoner, a malefactor, and was to be tried for his life for his escape. He was very loving and kind to us, and let friends go themselves to Bridgenorth, about fourteen miles, where the assizes were then held; and he desired me to stay with him in his affliction, and not be much from him. He said his life was at stake, and if God and the judge would shew him any mercy, he said, it was upon our friends' account, and not for any deserts that were in himself, for he confessed he had been too severe to us; but notwithstanding, said he, you are merciful men, and can forgive wrongs and injuries.

When we came to Bridgenorth, we were put in a large spacious room in the house of correction, to be there in the day-time, that we might be all together, and ready when called for; but we had liberty of going in and out for lodging, and what necessaries we wanted; no keeper being over us, but what we set ourselves to look to the door, and that too many friends might not be out at once, and those were not to stay out too long. We saw it was convenient, that friends should go out by two and two, to walk the streets; for it was a strange thing to people to hear of Quakers. Once it fell to my lot to be at the door, (though the door was always open, that such who would, might come and see us; with several of whom we had reasonings and disputes about the way of truth and righteousness) there came one, who appeared something like a gentleman, and asked me, whether he might see the Quakers; I desired him to walk up along with me, and he should see them. When I had brought him up to the room where friends were walking, I told him, those were they. He answered, these be Christians like ourselves, but where are the Quakers? I told him, these were they that were called Quakers. He asked me, whether I was one of them; I told him, I was one so called. I had an opportunity to declare to him the way of truth, and that the name of Quaker was given to us in scorn and derision; and he departed very friendly. Some people were so blind and dark in those days, that they looked upon us to be some strange creatures, and not like other men and women. They would gather much about us in the town, and we had good opportunities to speak of the things of God to them. But I was pretty much with the jailor, waiting when his trial would be; and when it came, I went with him, and stood somewhat near him, which he was very glad of. The jury cleared him, being not found guilty of a wilful escape; which was gladness to him, and satisfaction to us. And when the assizes was near at an end, the judge returned us to one justice Holland, except William Gibson, to whom the judge put it, whether he would go home, if he were discharged; but he could not make the judge such a promise as he required, so he was committed again to the same prison; but we were freely and friendly discharged, having had good service in that town, and the Lord was with us, and brought us safe home, to the comfort of our families and ourselves; and we have cause to bless and praise the name of the Lord, for ever, for all his mercies and goodness to us all along, in the time of our afflictions and persecutions. We could say, surely God is good to Israel and unto all them that draw nigh unto him with an upright heart.

CHAPTER IV.

A MEETING AT DOLOBRAN—LORD HERBERT OF CHIRBURY—CHARLES LLOYD IMPRISONED—LETTER TO THE QUARTER SESSIONS—TRUTH SPREADING IN MERIONETH—VAVASOR POWELL'S LAMENT—JAMES PARKES ADDRESSES PROFESSORS AT WREXHAM----RICHARD DAVIES'S TESTIMONY AT THE STEEPLE HOUSE—THE HIRELING FLEES.

In the year 1662, a farther concern came upon me about meetings, in this country. One that was convinced in the prison of Montgomery, when I was there, viz. Cadwalader Edwards, who lived near Dolobran, promised me that we should have his house to keep a meeting in. I went to know whether he would perform his promise, which he readily granted; and I appointed the day and time with him, which he gave notice of to his neighbours thereabouts. I being destitute of a friend to accompany me to the meeting, depended upon the Lord, that he would provide a suitable companion to go with me. And my wife going to Shrewsbury, I told her of the meeting, and desired her to speak to friends there of it, that if there was any public friend there, he might come home along with her. There happened to be Richard Moor, of Salop, a worthy and faithful labourer in the gospel, who came along with her to our house in Welch-Pool. This was in the ninth month, 1662. A day or two after, we went to the meeting, where came in Charles Lloyd, of

Dolobran, who was formerly in commission of the peace, and had been in election to be high-sheriff of that county, and also several of his well meaning neighbours, some of them were professors, belonging to the same people that I formerly belonged to. The Lord was not wanting, but afforded unto us his good presence; life and power came from him, that reached to the hearts and understandings of most of the people then present, who gave testimony to the truth, life and power of God, that appeared with us that time; and in the love, fear, and life of truth we parted.

The next morning we went to visit Charles Lloyd,* of Dolobran, who tenderly received us, and several that were at the meeting, came there that day; where we had a sweet, comfortable, refreshing time, in the presence of the Lord; as it is said, "In his presence is fulness of joy, and at his right hand, there are pleasures for evermore." Psal. xvi. 11.

The report of this meeting went through the country, some saying, that most of that side of the country were turned Quakers. Whereupon divers were sent for, before Edward Lord Herbert, Baron of Chirbury, to a place where he then lived, called Llyssin, about three miles from Dolobran. After some discourse with them, he sent them to Welch-Pool to prison, for refusing to take the oath of allegiance and supremacy, which they refused, because they could not swear at all; they being about six sent together, viz. Charles Lloyd, Hugh David, Richard David, Cadwalader Edwards, Annie Lawrence, Sarah Wilson, &c. where they were continued very close prisoners.

In a little time were added prisoners to them, William Lewis, and Margaret his wife, who were owners of the

---

* An ancestor of the Lloyds of Birmingham.

house at Cloddiaucochion, before-mentioned, where I was moved to go, about the year 1657, to a meeting of the professors, afterwards the place of my abode. This William Lewis, my near relation, was he that led me out of the house to the common, and shut the gate against me, as before related, page 35. And thus the word of the Lord was fulfilled, that came to me then, that those people should own and receive truth, and that house should be a meeting-house for us, which it now is, and hath been these forty years.

The oath of allegiance and supremacy being tendered to them, they could not take it for conscience sake; swearing at all being forbidden by Christ and his apostle James; so they were sent to prison, and continued prisoners there. Edward Evans also, an honest and substantial man, was committed to prison for the same supposed offence, who was convinced some time before; I having had some weighty discourse with him about the things of God. He told me, when he was in prison with Vavasor Powell, with many more of their brethren in Pool jail, that Vavasor leaning upon a window of their prison opening to the street, saw me and my dear wife pass by, and said, behold Zacharias and Elizabeth; it was said of them, that they walked in all the commandments of God blameless. This Edward Evans, and some others of the prisoners, looking out through the window, saw us two called Quakers, that he and others a little before had preached severely against. They looked upon it, that the Lord had forced him to give that testimony of us, and several of them, as Edward Evans said, were convinced by that testimony of his concerning us; and in some time after came to live in obedience to the truth, and suffered for it.

These prisoners were kept very close, some of them were substantial freeholders, who were put in a dirty, nasty place near the stable and house of office, being a low room; the felons and other malefactors in a chamber over head, the chamber-pots and excrements, &c. often falling upon them. Charles Lloyd, who was a little before in commission of the peace, was put in a little smoky room, and did lie upon a little straw himself for a considerable time; and at length his tender wife Elizabeth, that was of a considerable family, (daughter of Sampson Lort, near Pembroke in South Wales) was made willing to lie upon straw with her dear and tender husband. And thus they both, with the rest of friends, did rather "choose to suffer affliction with the people of God, than to enjoy the pleasures of sin for a season."

I staid at home with them for some time, keeping our meetings in prison; but at length the jailor had strict charge to keep me from among them, alleging, that I strengthened them in their way and principles; and when the jailor kept me out, I went to a neighbour's back yard, having leave of him to see them, and speak with them.

The sufferings of friends being now very great, and still increasing, they sent the following paper to the quarter-sessions held at Montgomery.

To the Justices and Magistrates of this County of Montgomery.

"FORASMUCH as it is not unknown to you, that we, who by the scorners of this world (that know not God) are called Quakers, are detained and kept close prisoners, only for the testimony of a good conscience towards God and man, our friends not being suffered to visit us, though drunkards, liars, thieves and robbers, are not debarred of their friends' admittance to them. This unheard of cruelty, were enough itself to establish us in our ways, if they were never so erroneous, as you say. This we are persuaded in our hearts, that never did Christ, nor any of his apostles, use this, or any other way of cruelty, or persecution, to convince any of their errors, but contrariwise, by sound doctrine, and good conversation, and 'doing unto others, as they would they should do unto them,' for that was the rule that Christ left to true Christians.

" Now consider, in the soberness of your hearts and spirits, that if you were in our condition, would not you desire your enlargement? And seeing it is the king's clemency, in a declaration bearing date the 26th day of December, 1662, wherein he says, he is glad to lay hold on this occasion, to re-establish and renew unto all his subjects concerned in those promises, indulged by a true tenderness of conscience. This assurance and confirmation of his promise made at Breda, upon the word of a king, viz.

" We do declare all liberty to tender consciences, and that no man shall be disquieted, or called in question for differences of opinions in matters of religion." And moreover he saith, in the same declaration, as for what concerns the penalties upon those, who living peaceably, do not conform thereunto through scruple and tenderness of misguided consciences, but modestly, without scandal, perform their devotions in their own way. We understand by these words, viz. that it is his fatherly care, to publish this his declaration, to stop and prevent all other acting, according to former acts made against liberty of tender consciences. And we hope that you will be as favourable to us, your neighbours, (seeing power is committed to your hands) as the king, being chief magistrate, is unto his subjects,. These things have we seen fit and convenient to lay before you, that you may understand we are not ignorant of the king's clemency towards us.

And we (whose names are underwritten) do wait the fulfilling and performing this one other word more of a king, by you who profess yourselves to be his obedient and loyal subjects; notwithstanding all which former words and promises of the king, the supreme magistrate, we have been persecuted more by you, his inferior magistrates in this county, than in many other counties. And farther, that you may be left without excuse for that, if you do persecute us, it is without any cause from us, or any order from the supreme magistrate, the king of England.† If you do justice herein, the Lord will bless you; if not, sin will lie at your door.

"These from your friends, that desire the good and welfare of your souls and bodies, that have received the spirit of meekness; that can pray for them that persecute us, and despitefully use us, who in patience and long-suffering are content to submit to the will of God, who renders to every man according to the deeds done in the flesh."

Humphrey Wilson,
Richard Lewis,
Edward Evans,
Charles Lloyd,
Hugh David,
William Lewis,

Sarah Wilson,
Margaret Lewis,
Catherine Evans,
Annie Lawrence,

The foregoing paper was sent to the magistrates at their quarter-sessions, held at Montgomery, the 5th day of the eleventh month, 1662.

---

† However much the King may have been inclined to clemency, the Church of England Party—the Church defenders of that day made him do their pleasure by assenting to cruel and wicked laws, intended to coerce dissenters into the form and profession of the dominant sect.

A copy of it also was sent to the chief justices at Ludlow by the jailer, together with another paper directed to them.

A little time after this I went to Penllyn,* near Bala, in Merionethshire, to visit some friends and tender professors there, who received me kindly, and there I settled a meeting among them, in the power of God; and from thence I came home, where I staid but a little while, to visit these prisoners. Soon after I went to the house of Owen Lewis, at Tyddyn y Garreg, near Dolgelly, in Merionethshire, a man that had been in commission of the peace in Oliver's days, and was newly come from prison from Bala, who received me kindly, (he was first convinced by Thomas Briggs.)† From thence I went to Robert Owen's, of Dolserau, near Dolgelly, who had also been a justice of the peace, and a commander in Oliver's time. He received me and my testimony; as did also Owen Humphrey of Llwyngwril, near the seaside in the said county, (who was a justice of the peace in Oliver's days) and his father, his brothers Samuel and John Humphrey. These, with many more there, received the truth in the love of it, and continued faithful, serviceable men in their country, kept meetings in their houses, and many were gathered to the Lord among the rocks and mountains in those parts; this was in the year 1662. After this journey, the Lord brought me safe home to my wife and family, to the comfort of friends, and one another in the Lord.

Not long after this, Thomas Lloyd, brother to Charles

---

* I conclude that this Penllyn is another name for Llanuwchllyn.

† Thomas Briggs, who was convinced by Geo. Fox, at Lancaster in 1652, from being an opposer, became a diligent minister of the Word, and was fined five times for holding meetings in his house; he was very instrumental in turning men from darkness to Light; travelled much in Wales and accompanied Geo. Fox to the West Indies in 1671.

See Geo. Fox's Journal, 7th ed., p. 139

Lloyd, of Dolobran, hearing his brother was in prison, came from Oxford to visit him, having been a student there several years (as also his brother Charles had been before him) they told me that the great sufferings of friends, in that city of Oxford, by the magistrates, and by the wild and ungodly scholars,* did work much upon them; and they had some secret love for friends then. So when Thomas Lloyd came home, being some time with friends in prison, and elsewhere, the Lord opened his understanding by his light, life and power, and he received the truth and was obedient to it, took up his daily cross, and followed Jesus, came to be his disciple, was taught by him, and went no more to Oxford for learning; and I may say with David, "The Lord made him wiser than all his teachers." He staid pretty much at home, and with his eldest brother Charles Lloyd, and in these parts.

The jailer of Welch-Pool was very cruel to friends, and continued them in that nasty hole before-mentioned, till Edward Evans fell sick, by reason of the dampness and unhealthiness of the room, and died; and the jailer would not suffer us to have his body to be buried, except we would pay the coroner, and so clear him, as if he had no hand in his death; but at last his relations prevailed without a coroner's inquest, and they took and buried him on a hill, and the back-side of the steeple-house in Welch-Pool; and it happened, as they were digging the grave, they found some bones of a man, and upon enquiry in some old records, it was said, there was an old judge buried there; and the name of that place is called ever

---

* Oxford was then, as now, a breeding place of nettles, *spiritually*, and it will be so, as long as it is a training ground for men to preach for hire, or trust to any other qualification than the immediate call and baptism of the Spirit of Truth.

since, Judges Hill. We had got no burying-place of our own then, but were about having one.

Thomas Lloyd and I not being prisoners now, (though except us two) most that were then convinced were prisoners; the report of such who were turned Quakers being spread abroad, they were soon sent for before a magistrate, and the oath of allegiance and supremacy was tendered both to men and women; and they for conscience-sake refusing it, were sent to prison in order to be premunired.*

My friend Thomas Lloyd and I were moved to go and visit most of the justices that had a hand in committing friends to prison; we began at the farthest justice towards Machynlleth, and came down to Edward, Lord Herbert, Baron of Chirbury, at Llyssin aforesaid, who had committed Charles Lloyd, and several other friends; we understood on the way, that he was at a bowling-green, and several with him, near a place called the Cann Office, near the highway side, and not far from Llyssin, where we beheld them bowling. We considered with each other, which way to take, there being a peevish priest, the said lord's chaplain with them; so I asked Thomas Lloyd, whether he would engage the priest in discourse, or go to the said lord; which he chose, and got into the green leisurely towards him, where most of them knew Thomas; but he went not in their complimenting posture. He staid there but a little while, and they broke up their game, and while he discoursed with the Lord

---

* Those who refused to take the oaths of allegiance and supremacy, stood in danger of a sentence of PREMUNIRE, such as was pronounced against Francis Howgill, a faithful Christian minister, in 1674. "You are put out of the King's protection, and the benefit of the law, your lands are confiscated to the King during your life, and your goods and chattels for ever, and you to be a prisoner during your life."

The last clause was illegal as will be seen later on.

Herbert, I discoursed a little with the priest. Lord Herbert coming towards the priest and me, he said to the priest, Mr. Jones, what have you got there? He answered, a Quaker, and haberdasher of hats, that lives in Welch-Pool. Oh! said Lord Herbert, I thought he was such an one, he keeps his hat upon the block. Then he intending and preparing to come down a great steep ditch, I stepped down to lend him my hand to help him; another priest would have stepped between me and him, but Lord Herbert refused the priest's help; and stopping a little, said to the priest, here is a brother that stands by will say, the blind leads the blind, and both will fall into the ditch. The priest was so drunk, that he could not stand by himself. This lord being a very big fat man, took my help to come down, so we went along with him towards his own house at Llyssin, laying the sufferings of our friends before him, and that their sufferings were for conscience-sakes towards God. He gave us no grant then for their enlargement, but we heard that he sent private instructions, and they had more liberty. The jailer had an empty house at the end of the town, and there he let friends go, which was a sweet convenient place near the fields, without any keeper over them, and they had the liberty of the town, and to go where they pleased, except to their own houses.

So Charles Lloyd took a house in town for him and his family to live in; and we kept our meetings in that house of the jailer's aforesaid, for several years. Most of friends by this time being under a premunire, many friends came from several places to visit them, and those that were convinced towards Machynlleth, William Evans, and several others of that end of the county (who were formerly Independents) were sent here to prison upon

---

* Edward Lord Herbert of Chirbury, grandson of the first lord who is known chiefly by his Autobiography.

the same account, refusing to take the oaths of allegiance and supremacy. Peter Price also, a worthy man of Radnorshire, was sent to this prison; he had been in commission of the peace in Oliver's days; he, with several others with him, were committed by the justices of this county, to the house of correction in Welch-Pool, for three months, as vagrants, because they came out of their own county Radnorshire, adjoining to this county of Montgomeryshire, where they remained the three months; but they had the liberty of the town, and to go to meetings with the rest of the prisoners. Other friends, that lived in and about the town, met with them in prison, and considerable meetings we had in that house.

A little after this, Thomas Ellis, called a deacon in the Independent congregation, was convinced: a man of great esteem among them, and so he was also amongst us. He came to my house to visit the prisoners, his former fellow church members, and showed me a letter that came to him from their minister, Vavasor Powell, lamenting the deplorable condition and danger they were in at that time; saying,* that the Christians were in great danger to be split between two rocks, that was the World and Q. (meaning the Quakers) but the worst, said he, is Q. But the Lord had opened Thomas Ellis's understanding, and given him a sight of their decay and formalities.

Some years before the Lord did break in among them, to the convincing of many of them; for Thomas told me, that there came two women friends among them, in the time of their breaking of their bread, (I

---

* What Vavasor Powell really did say, we gather more nearly from the Welsh edition of Richard Davies' life, pub. 1840—Dywedai yn ei lythyr fod y Cristionogion mewn mawr berygl o hollti rhwng dwy graig; sef y Byd a'r C (gan feddwl y Crynwyr) ond y waethaf ebai efe oedd y C.

suppose it was before I came from London) and when they had the motion of truth upon them, they opened their mouths in the name of the Lord, in much fear and humility; so that the Independent elders stood still and gave the women leave to speak what they had to say to the people; then the professers went on again with their business, and after some time the friends spoke again; and then they commanded them to be taken away, but none was very ready to do it. Then their minister, Vavasor Powell, called,—Brother Ellis, take them away. Thomas Ellis told me, that he remembered Christ was not hasty in passing sentence upon the woman, that the Jews brought before him in the case of adultery; but he stooped down, and wrote with his finger upon the ground, as though he heard them not. So T. Ellis told me he was not willing to take them away, till they had fully cleared themselves of what was upon them to deliver among them: but at last they called to him again, and bid him take them away. Then he rose from among the company and went to them, and desired them to go with him to the next room, for he had something to say to them, and the friends went readily with him; then he told them in this wise: Friends, you see how we are met together here; we are like the Prodigal, who was spending his portion, and we have a little yet unspent; and when we have spent all, we must return to our heavenly Father, and come to you and your way. The friends went away well satisfied. I have made much enquiry who these friends were, and from whence they came, but could not certainly learn who they were. As for our friend Thomas Ellis, the Lord blessed him, and poured his spirit upon him, and gave him part of the ministry, and he became a faithful labourer and serviceable man among us; and at length he was made a prisoner here at Welch-Pool.

About the year 1663, our friend James Parkes came from the north, hearing that some of his acquaintance and fellow church members owned truth ;* he came to give them a visit in the love of God, and also to visit those Independents he formerly walked among that were not convinced ; and he left a paper with me to deliver to to them, which was thus :

---

* By the expression "owned Truth," we understand that these persons had separated themselves from a form of worship performed in man's will and time, and in some degree at least, were identified with the despised Quakers. It is not unreasonable to suppose that most of such around Wrexham, had been members of the congregation of Morgan Llwyd (spelt Floydd mentioned in Geo. Fox's Journal).

The history of the Friend's Congregation, if there was one at this period, is somewhat obscure, but it would appear probable from the way in which Hugh Morus of Llansilin alludes to Quakers, that old soldiers of the Commonwealth occasionally embraced spiritual religion in Wales as was the case in England.

    Y *foru* fe ae 'n *Drwper*,† i beidio â'i bader,
    A *thrennydd* yn *Gwacer*, oer egr ei rudd ;
    Fel *mwrdrwr* pen-isel, heb gyfarch na *ffarwel*,
    Un ddull ag anifail anufudd.
                      Eos Ceiriog Cyf I., t. 211.

It would also appear that women's preaching was not unknown in Denbighshire in Oliver's days, (see Carol Gwyliau a wnaed yn amser rhwysg Olifer) and we can hardly doubt that it proceeded from those who had themselves received the ministration of the Day Spring from on high which qualifies male or female to speak or prophesy in the Divine name, just when and how it will

Huw Morus's contemptuous reference to the Quakers and women's preach ng proceeded from darkness, and ignorance of the further light on Divine things, which was then spreading in this country, bringing back religion to its original pure foundation, in a way contrary to human wisdom. In consequence he grossly belied and travested the retired and serious demeanour of the Children of the Light.

† A Trooper.

A Lamentation and Warning from the Lord God, in the love of Christ Jesus, unto all the Professors in North Wales, especially those about Wrexham in Denbighshire, and Welch-Pool in Montgomeryshire, whom formerly I have known, and walked with, in a fellowship and worship, till the Lord awakened me out of sleep, and opened in me a ear to hear his Voice, which cried, Come out from amongst them, and be thou separate; touch no unclean thing, and I will receive thee.

"Friends,

"Hear and lend an ear, O ye professors of Wrexham and Welch-Pool, and all the places and towns adjacent thereunto, who have been called churches of Christ, and members of his body, and followers of the Lamb. I am come in my Father's name to visit you, and in bowels of his love, in this the day of your calamity and adversity have I visited many of you, in obedience to his command, who sent me in his name and fear into these parts, chiefly for your sakes at this time, that you might hear, and come to fear him, whose voice hath shaken the earth, and removed it out of its place: and he is making the keepers of the house to tremble, and he hath bound the strong man in many, that was armed, and formerly kept the house, then all was at peace; but a stronger than he is risen, and manifest in the hearts of thousands, even Christ Jesus, the Light of the world, who enlighteneth every one that cometh into the world, that all in him, and through him, might believe. He is dividing the spoil, and spoiling principalities and powers; and they whose eyes come to see him the Lord of Hosts, come to be undone. When Moses saw the appearance of the Lord, he did exceedingly fear and quake. It was he that made Habbakuk tremble, and his lips to quiver. And whosoever comes to know Christ, must know him through death, be baptised into his death, and suffer with him, before they come to live and reign with him. They must repent of all their wickedness, and turn from it, before they can come to be assured of rest and peace. Let none think God will wink at their wickedness, as he did in the times of ignorance; for now he is leaving all without excuse, and calling every man to repent. The light is risen, that manifests sin and hypocrisy in them that hold truth in unrighteousness, it is not the name of being called church-members, will serve any of your turns.

" O ye professors of all sorts, from the highest to the lowest, from the richest to the poorest; I am moved of the Lord God to warn you, that while you have time and space, you may be redeemed out of all evil; and that you might come out from amongst evil-doers, and so be saved from the wrath and destruction that will overtake the workers of iniquity, who repent not of their evil deeds, to give God the glory; and with the whirlwind of his wrath, he will vex you in his sore displeasure. O ye professors of Christ, and the apostle's words! who are not come to his life, nor to be of the same mind that he was of, who endured the contradiction of sinners, and was made perfect through sufferings; whom the apostles bore testimony to, and suffered for; being of the same mind, they did not shrink nor bow, nor let go their testimony, when persecution arose because of the word; but they overcame by the blood of the Lamb, and by the word of his testimony, which they held; and they loved not their lives unto death.—Are you all so blind, that you cannot see yourselves to be out of the light and image of Christ, and out of their practice, who followed him, and confessed him, and did not deny him before men; neither did they change their religion, as the powers of the earth changed. For whatsoever the powers of the earth countenanced, or discountenanced, they mattered not, who were of the true church that were of God, the Father of our Lord Jesus Christ, the pillar and ground of truth ; but that which God made manifest to be his will, that they did ; and though they were charged, by the powers that were then, to speak no more in his name, yet they spoke in his name, and did not deny his name.

" Dare you say, that you are saints, and of this church of Christ, and yet live in the breach of his commandments, who said, ' Swear not at all ; ' as some more eminent in esteem amongst you have done, and have taught others to do ? Doth not the land mourn because of swearing ? Are not such like the Scribes and Pharisees, who would not enter into the kingdom of heaven themselves, nor suffer them that would to enter in ? Are not such now shutting the kingdom of heaven against men ? And must not the woes from the Lord be pronounced against them? Yea, assuredly, and will overtake them; pain shall suddenly come upon them, as on a travailing woman, and they shall not escape it. The Lord is come to deliver his people out of the teeth of these devourers, who with good words and fair speeches have deceived the hearts of some more simple and honest amongst you, and made merchandise of them, by promising you peace, while you are in your wicked ways and works; which the true prophets and apostles of old, whom the Lord sent, could not do ; neither can they, who are of the same descent, royal seed, and off-spring now ; they know, there is no peace to be spoken to any, while they are in their wicked ways, drinking up iniquity as the ox drinketh water. Oh ! my heart is broken within me, and I cannot but take up a lamentation for you, who have been esteemed beautiful, and the glory of many that have been called churches, to see you carried away captive, by the prince of the power of the air, that ruleth in the children of disobedience; and that you should be yet lying under the bondage of corruption and in sin, the wages whereof is death; out of the glorious liberty of the sons of God; and that death should reign over you, subjecting you to the power of the enemy; and you are taken captive by him at his will, laden with sins, and led away with divers lusts, like the silly women spoken of in the scriptures of truth, that were ever learning, and never able to come to the knowledge of the truth, but resist it; and so err in your minds, not knowing the scriptures, nor the power of God, though you talk of them. If you knew the scriptures, and the power of God, which brings into the life of them, you would witness the ability the saints in former times had, and now the saints of the Most High have, to stand over the powers of darkness, hell and death; then you would come to that which cannot be shaken, nor the gates of hell prevail against you.—But have not the powers of darkness prevailed against you, overcome you, and made you bow to their will, and to their laws, that will bind the conscience, and hinder its full liberty?

"Oh! consider seriously, and weigh in the coolness of your spirits, and in the fear of the Lord, what you have done; whether you have not received the beast's mark, either in your foreheads or in your hands: have you not fainted in the day of adversity? Have you not let go the profession of your faith, and wavered in your minds? Have you not licked up your old vomits again; Are you not wallowing in the filth of iniquity, and in your fleshy minds, walking in the sensuality and in the carnal mind, which is enmity against God? Is it not death to be carnally minded? Are they not in death that are in the carnal mind? It is not strange to me, if I find such an enmity: because I expect no other from natural men, who perceive not the things of the spirit. You have rejected the chief corner-stone, which is laid in Sion for a foundation, and have not believed in the Light of the world, who is become the Head-stone in God's building and husbandry, and of the church that is pure, without spot or wrinkle, which is in God, the Father of our Lord Jesus Christ, the pillar and ground of truth. This is the city sought out, not forsaken. This is the habitation of God through the spirit, the stones whereof are laid with fair colours, the foundation of sapphire, and all the borders of pleasant stones. Such being redeemed out of sin, and from under the bondage of corruption cannot plead for it, as some, looked upon amongst you more than others, do; and would endeavour to make you believe, that the prophet Isaiah was always a man of unclean lips; but that was before he was undone, and while the woe was upon him. Ah, brutish is that spirit that would imagine, that our God should make use of a man to do so much for his name and honour, as Isaiah did, and yet continue a man of unclean lips. This I testify, that Isaiah's iniquity was taken away, and his sins purged out. Such manifest themselves to be ignorant of Christ's death and manifestations, which is to take away sin, and in him is no sin. All that come to him in his light, and to walk in it, have fellowship one with another, and the blood of Jesus Christ cleanseth them from all sin. Such come by him to be made free from sin, and servants to righteousness; not of sin; for sin and iniquity comes to be done away; and then God beholds no iniquity in Jacob, nor transgression in Israel; and to such is given the tongue of the learned, to speak a word in due season to the weary. Such come to know the pure language, which the Lord promised to turn to his people. Such set a watch before their mouths, and have a bridle for their tongue. Now some plead for uncleanness, because the prophet said, he was a man of unclean lips, before he was touched with the lively coal, and before his iniquity was done away, and his sins purged out; and assuredly one day you shall all know that this is a false cover, too narrow to cover yourselves with, who break the commandments of Christ, and teach others so to do; and that put your hands to the plough, and look back: so that your are not fit for the kingdom of heaven. You are filled with your own ways, wicked devices, and false covers you get to cover yourselves withal; but all your false coverings will prove too narrow, and your beds of ease, and false rests, which you think to stretch yourselves upon, too short: and no rest or peace there shall you have, but you shall all yet be farther tried, and your folly be made more manifest; and all the false covers, all professors out of the life and power of God have been covered with, shall be plucked off; yea, all that are covered, and not with the Spirit of the Lord. The woe is to them who are adding sin to sin, and are not come to cleanness of heart, or cleanness of lips; and as long as you are in the uncleanness, and the best of you, as a brier pleading for it, blush for shame! Relinquish the title of church-membership, till you come to tread in the steps of Christ, and obey him; for his servants ye are to whom ye obey. Deceive yourselves no longer with the name of Christians only, but come to the nature, to witness the first old nature and birth slain, and brought under; which you all must do, before ever you come to know the new nature, or birth that is of the spirit; for that which is born of the flesh, that is flesh; and that which is born of the spirit, that is spirit. If any man be in Christ, he is a new creature; old things are passed away, and all things are become new. The church of Christ is made up of living stones, squared and hewed into order, complete together, made a spiritual household, purged, washed, and made white, and the filth of the flesh done away. Such come to be vessels of honour, fit for the Master's use, receive of the heavenly treasure into the earthen vessel, and out of the abundance of the treasury of the heart, bring forth good things. With the heart man believeth unto righteousness; and with the mouth confession is made unto salvation.

"So every one come to Him that searcheth the heart, trieth the reins, and will reward every one according to their works, or deeds done in the body, whether they be good or evil; for the Lord God will be no longer mocked, such as you sow you must reap; he will no longer bear your halt and blind service, and dead worships, out of the life and power of God. Your hypocrisy and dissimulation is seen by the Spirit of truth, that leads and guides into all truth, which you shall one day know is now striving with you, as it did with them before the flood; yet shall not always strive with men. It saith, who requireth these things at your hands? And do you think God is pleased, or will now be served with the dry, dead and airy service and worships? I tell you nay; the light of the glorious gospel is manifest, and the pearl of great price is found, and many have sold, and parted with all which was most dear to them, and which they most delighted in, to buy it; and they who come to believe in Christ Jesus, the Light, the Way, the Truth, the Life, and to walk in the light, they stumble not nor stagger at the promises; but come to have life in themselves, and their minds, words, and actions are seasoned. They are the salt of the earth, a city set on a hill, that cannot be hid, and their lights shine so before men, that they who are not wilfully blind, may see their good works, and godly conversation coupled with fear; and they that walk in the light, as he is in the light, have fellowship one with another, and the blood of Christ they witness, cleansing them from all sin. So if ever you come to know God aright, you must turn to the light that reproves you for evil, for the reproof of instruction is the way to life; and they that hate that which reproves them for their evil deeds, and sets their sins in order before men, abide in the chambers of death, and know not rest, life, and peace for their souls. Now as you come to the light, and wait in the light which comes from Christ, all your sins will be set in order before you, and it will shew you all that ever you did; as you shall one day know, to your woe and misery, if you continue rejecting him. This is He in whom we believe, and of whom the prophets and apostles bore witness, whose name is better than every name, unto which every knee must bow, and every tongue confess; and every tongue that would rise up in judgment against him, shall be condemned, and shall fall before him.

"Therefore beware, and take heed what you do; repent of all your evil deeds, of all your hard speeches which you have uttered against him, and his glorious appearance in his sons and daughters, in this the day of his power, wherein He hath made many willing to follow him wheresoever he goeth, even through many tribulations, who have washed their robes in the blood of the Lamb; when you deny him, and will follow him no farther than it will make with your peace in the world, and enjoyment of your pleasures, and keep the friendship and favour of the world, which none ever did, but who were adulterated from the life of God, and turned against the pure spirit in themselves; and this shall you know.

"So whether you will hear or forbear, in this I shall have peace. My reward is with God, in that I have discharged my duty, and warned you before your day be quite over, before the Lord leave off stretching forth his hand, who knows and searches the hearts of all men;

who knows my love towards you all, and to that which is pure of him, which never consented to sin, in all your consciences; even to that, and nothing else, can I, or desire I, to be made manifest. I believe there is a seed to be brought forth from amongst you, which must be gathered into the true fold of everlasting rest and peace; for which seed's sake I travail night and day, waiting for its redemption and restoration, who am your friend, who seeks not yours but you; that you might come to know in this your day, the things that concern your everlasting peace, comfort, and true settlement, (upon that rock that cannot be shaken, nor the gates of hell ever prevail against) before they be hidden from your eyes. Knowing the terrors of the Lord, and the wrath that is to be revealed from heaven against all that hold truth in unrighteousness; and having obtained mercy from the Lord, and in his name, the strong tower, hid myself, I cannot but persuade all to come into the same; and being in a deep sense in the loving-kindness of the Lord, and what he hath done for my soul, since I walked with you, and was esteemed one of you, too large here to relate; neither indeed am I able to demonstrate the loving-kindness of the Lord, in the visitation of his pure love, in turning me from darkness (which I must confess all the time I was with you, I walked in) into his marvellous light, and from the power of Satan, unto God. He hath made me to feel and witness his power, wherein, through his good will towards me, I have found the ability to perform and to do the good, that when I was amongst you I desired to do; and likewise to resist the evil that I would not do. This is the Lord's own doing, and it is marvellous in my eyes; and I desire never to forget the Lord's great love to me, and powerful effectual working in me, to will and to do of his own good pleasure. I desire not to eat my morsel alone; but that all may come to taste and see how good the Lord is. Great and marvellous are his works, just and true are all his ways, he waits to be gracious, and there is no want to them that fear the Lord. He never forsakes nor doth withhold any good thing from them that walk uprightly.

"So, friends, while you have time, prize it, and put not the day of the Lord far from you, for the Lord is not slack concerning his promise, as some men count slackness; but his long-suffering is not for any to perish, but that all shall come to repentance. Now is the day that every man's works must be tried, and every man's faith and love to God will be tried. Now is the day that many great professors make shipwreck of their faith, and of a good conscience, and some that formerly seemed somewhat tender and honest amongst you, are grown sottish and brutish, and their understandings darkened, through the ignorance that is in them. The god of this world hath blinded the eyes of many great professors, by keeping them from the light, by which they might see their ways, and the works which they are doing out of the light, in the blindness which hath happened to them; but if you would come to the light, which is pure, of God in you, then would he receive power to perform the acceptable will and requirings of the Lord; which that you may come to know and do, is the desire of your friend, that seeks not yours but you; and desires your everlasting peace and happiness, who formerly was known, and esteemed of, as a brother amongst you, by the name of JAMES PARKES."

Wrexham, the 9th of the
first month, 1662.

Several friends, both from the North and South of England, were drawn to visit these friends in prison, and many sweet and comfortable epistles were written to them.

There was a great convincement in the year 1662, in these two counties, viz. Montgomeryshire, and Merionethshire; and as meetings increased, several friends came into Welch-Pool, where our meeting was kept in that house that was their prison. The magistrates and priest were discontented, some saying, that there came as many to the meeting, as went to their worship at the church, as they called it.

So the magistrates were resolved to come and break up our meeting, and one first day they came, viz., Thomas Corbet, a counsellor and a justice of peace in this county, together with two bailiffs of the town, the serjeants at mace and under officers. When they came into the meeting I was at prayer, and they were indifferently civil till I had concluded, and then began to take our names. When they had done, my wife called to justice Corbet, and told him, they had not taken the names of all that were at the meeting; he asked her, who was untaken; and she put her child towards him, about a quarter old. He said, That was under age. She answered, We are all as innocent from plotting, contriving, or thinking any harm to any man, as this child; which smote much this Thomas Corbet, and several others present. They committed me to one serjeant's house; and Thomas Lloyd, brother to Charles Lloyd, and Samuel Lloyd, (son to Samuel Lloyd of Dudson, in the county of Salop, eldest brother to John and David Lloyd, of London, and Edward Lloyd of Bristol) to the other serjeant's house. When the serjeant, whose house I was committed to, was come from the steeplehouse, he turned me out, and bid me go home, I should not stay there. So I went first to see my friends the old prisoners, who were kept, for a little time, more close, and we were not suffered to go to them; they were very glad to see me, and I was refreshed also to see them, though we could not go to one another. In a little time, I went to see the other two prisoners, that were at the other serjeant's house, and the serjeant let them come home with me.

On second-day following, it came into my mind, that the magistrates would try us with an offer, to pass by that which they called a transgression, upon condition that we would go to the steeple-house to their worship the next first-day following; which I told to friends.

On third-day following, justice Corbet, and the two bailiffs that had committed us to prison, sent for us before them. So we went, Thomas Lloyd, Samuel Lloyd, and myself. After some discourse with them, they proposed to us, that if we would go to church and hear divine service, as they called it, we should be discharged. I told them, when I was last there, they turned me out of their church, and if I should make any promise to go there, it may be they would do the like by me again. Justice Corbet said, He would engage I should not be turned out. Then I told them I knew nothing to the contrary, but that I would come there. Justice Corbet seemed to be satisfied; but one of the bailiffs said, Mr. Corbet, do you think that the old Quaker will come to church, except it be to disturb our minister? Corbet asked me again, Whether I would disturb the minister? I told him, if God should put something in my heart to speak to the people,* I hope they would not impose upon me to hold my peace. He said, God forbid they should do so! Then I told him, I hoped I should perform what I had promised to do; and so they discharged us. Now none was under an engagement to go to the steeple-house but myself, and the report went about that the old Quaker would go to church.

---
* This would simply be making use of Apostolic liberty which priestcraft has taken away.

The reader will observe in the following paragraph that Richard Davies and his friends speak of the steeple-house rather than of the church, Why? For this reason; Christianity leads into simplicity and truth, and not into confusion. A church is not bricks and mortar, but a gathering or congregation of people; a Christian Church is a gathering of faithful men and women, *i.e.*, those who are in good measure faithful to the light and grace they have received from God—the church of God is the whole company of redeemed and purified spirits, and those yet in the shackles of mortality, whose faith and dependance is in the same living Spirit which is the light and life of men, and whereby alone they can worship aright. But note the artfulness of priestcraft! It is not enough for hireling priests that human souls should be taught to pray to God in the Spirit, and learn to take their part in the one true church universal—Babylon the great with all her wares and merchandise would fall, fall, fall in that day and be counted as nothing; so the idea is inculcated that the presence of God is peculiarly to be found in certain buildings supposed to be consecrated or made holier than other buildings by a magical ceremony, and henceforth entitled to be honoured by the name church. Thus, the poor laity are tempted to offer an exterior homage, while the temple of the heart which should be a place of prayer remains a " den of thieves."

When first-day came, and the bells began to ring, the other two friends, viz. Thomas Lloyd, and Samuel Lloyd, came to me and said, we think we must go with thee to the steeple-house. When the people went to the steeple-house, I took my bible under my arm, and went to

G

justice Corbet's house, (that was but a few doors from my house) to let him see that I was going, and I asked him, whether he was coming? He said, He was not disposed to come that day, but he would send his man to see we were not affronted. So the two friends and I went to my own pew, that was opposite to the pulpit. There was but the curate to read the common-prayer, and their service to them that morning; there was a great multitude of people: some said, there were some that had not been at their church several years before. So nothing was laid upon us* to speak to the people, till he had done. Then I stood up, and said to the people, I suppose you are not ignorant of the cause of our coming here this day, which was thus: the magistrates of the town came to our meeting, and they found us upon our knees praying to Almighty God. They were civil while we were at prayer, and when we had done, they took our names and committed us three to prison; most of the rest that were at the meeting were prisoners before. And the magistrates told us, If we would come to church, we should be discharged; and now you see we are come, according to their desire. But I find your priest is not here, and now I would have you inform him, that I say,

1. If he proves this to be the true Church of Christ;
2. And that he is a true minister of Christ;
3. And that his maintenance is a gospel-maintenance;
4. And this worship of yours to be the true worship of God;

Then we will be of your religion, and come again to you. †

But if he proves not this, then we must conclude,
1. Your church to be a false church;

---

* Note this—They did not go to disturb the curate in their own time, but waited till the Lord laid it in their spirit.

† A thoroughly fair offer.

2. And he to be no true minister of Christ;
3. That his maintenance is no gospel-maintenance;
4. That your worship is not the true worship of God.

All the people were very civil and orderly, and heard me a considerable while in the steeple-house. When I had done, Thomas Lloyd spoke a few very seasonable words to the people. And the people said, if Mr. Langford (which was the priest's name) will not prove us to be the true church of Christ, and our worship to be the true worship, then we will pay him no more tithes, for what Richard Davies said he proved out of the bible; for you see, he had the bible in his hand all the while. So for that time we parted.

When the bells rang again for them to go to their evening service, it lay upon me to go there again, and the aforesaid friends went along with me; where the old high-priest was, who made a long sermon, till we were all uneasy; but I desired the friends to bear all things patiently. When the priest had done, he was going away; but I stepped up in my seat, and desired him to stay, for I had something to say to him; which was the same as aforesaid: when he heard my queries, and what I had to say, he turned his back and went away, and gave us no answer. Then I said, behold the hireling fleeth, because he is an hireling. Some of the people staid, and some went with him, but all dissatisfied, that he would not prove them to be the true church of Christ, &c.* I had a good opportunity to speak to the people more at large in the graveyard; the Lord's presence, life, and power was with us, blessed be the

---

* It is to be desired that there were so much simplicity in people's minds, as even to wish to see it proved that the worship of the Church of England is the true worship of God. After a sincere search, the eyes of many would be opened to see that it is impossible, that any worship where man's will takes the lead should be so.

name of the Lord for ever, who doth not forsake his people that trust in him.

When we came home, justice Corbet sent for us again to him. He met us in his court, and said, he was sorry Mr. Langford was so uncivil, that he did not answer our queries, which, he thought, were very reasonable. In a little time, many of the neighbours were gathered together in the street, and in his court, we had a good opportunity to reason with him, and to open to the people, and declare to them the way and means to obtain the kingdom of heaven; and he was so moderate, that one of the neighbours said to him, Mr. Corbet, we think you will be a Quaker too. His answer was, I wish I were a Quaker in my life and conversation. Towards the end of our discourse, he desired me to give him my queries in writing, that Mr. Langford might answer them; for, said he, it may be he was not prepared to answer you then, but he may answer them in writing. I told him that was but a private way of answering; but if he was not prepared then, I told him we would give him the meeting next first-day at the steeple-house, or in the town-hall upon a market-day. He said, it was very fair.

Counsellor Corbet was very friendly and loving to us, and did no more persecute us to his dying day; but did us all the good he could, in all the courts of judicature where he was concerned.

As for this priest, William Langford, many friends were moved to go to him to the steeple-house in the time of his service, to declare to him and the people, what they had to say from the Lord; and when the magistrates have committed some of them to prion son that account, when their service was over, this priest* hath got them to be released.

---

* Although a hireling, he was evidently not without some respect for the nobility of Truth.

Some time after this, he sent the clerk of the parish to me for Easter-reckonings. I asked the clerk, whether his master did expect any thing of me, that had nothing from him; and bid him tell his master, I would come to reckon with him by and by. So the clerk went his way, And in a little time I made myself ready. When I went to him, there were a pretty many people with him. I told him, his clerk had been with me from him, for that which he called Easter-reckonings, and I was come to reckon with him, if he could make it appear that I owed him any thing, I would pay him, and I expected the same from him. He said, I owed him for several years for the sacrament. I asked him, what he meant by the word sacrament, for I found no such word in the scripture; he said, it meant the bread and wine which was used in the church. I told him, I received none of him, and was therefore not liable to pay. He answered again, why then you might come to church and receive it. I told him, I did not believe that church was the true church of Christ: and I did not believe he was a true minister of Christ, commissioned by him to break the bread, and give it to the people; much less to sell it, or take money for it of the people; for I did not read in all the scripture, that the true ministers of Christ did take money of the people for that bread they delivered unto them. He said then, that the labourer was worthy of his hire; and under the law it was said, "Thou shalt not muzzle the mouth of the ox that treadeth out the corn." I told him, he trod out no corn for me; and though he was an hireling, yet I never hired him.

The people coming thick to pay him for the bread and wine, I asked him, how in conscience he could take so much money for so little bread and wine; it being, I suppose, about ten pence for man and wife. I asked him, what scripture he had for it; and desired him to prove his practice by scripture. He asked me, what scripture I had to eat flummery. I told him, I had scripture to eat it. Paul said to Timothy, " For every creature of God is good, and nothing to be refused, if it be received with thanksgiving: for it is sanctified by the word of God and prayer," 1 Tim. iv. 4, 5. His communicants who were present, were much dissatisfied that he had no better answer and proof for his practice. So I desired the people to take notice, that he could not make it appear by scripture, that I owed him anything; but I told them, that he owed me some money, and I desired him to pay it me, which he did. So we parted fairly. We have a saying, that even, or often reckonings make long friends. He was very friendly afterwards, and never sent to me more for Easter-reckonings. And as for the tithe,* in time of harvest, he charged his servants to take from me no more than their due, nor so much. I was informed he should say, he knew not why he should take any thing from me, seeing I had nothing from him. He lived here among us many years, a good neighbour; and though in the time of great persecution, yet he had no hand in persecuting any of us.

We have cause to bless the Lord, who carried us through all our services and exercises, in the time of our weakness; and though we were little and low in our own eyes, the Lord did not leave us; blessed be his holy name for ever.

---

* Altogether, the character of Priest Langford in spite of his failings, contrasts well with that of some of the ecclesiastics and tithe owners of our day.

CHAPTER V.

THE SCHISM OF JOHN PERROT—RICHARD DAVIES BURDENED WITH UNANOINTED PREACHING—TESTIMONY AGAINST CADWALADER EDWARDS—MEETING AT ABERYSTWITH AND IMPRISONMENT OF RICHARD DAVIES— JOURNEY WITH JOHN AP JOHN—ROGER PRICHARD RESTORED—FRENCH BRETONS—CARDIFF—THE VILE INFORMER.

About the year 1663 or 1664, I went to London, and found some there separated from that love and unity, which I formerly saw them in; joining in that spirit with John Perrot,* who was newly come from prison at

---

* John Perrot was a man who became a sad Apostate from the Truth.

He went to Italy on a religious concern about the year 1660 with John Love, and was admitted to the palace of the Doge of Venice to whom he gave some books. At Rome they bore testimony against the Idolatry committed there and were taken into custody. John Love fell into the hands of the Inquisition, and it is reported was murdered. Perrot was put into the madhouse, whence he wrote sundry papers. The following is from the title of one of them published in 1660:—

" Battering Rams against Rome or the Battel of John the follower of the Lamb," fought with the Pope and his Priests whilst he was a prisoner in the Inquisition prison of Rome.

Also a certain " REMONSTRANCE OF RIGHTEOUS REASON " written in Rome Prison of Madmen unto all Rome's rulers.

Sewell the historian observes that he "not continuing in true humility, ran out into exorbitant imaginations." He afterwards went to America, wore gaudy apparel, and became a severe exactor of oaths, thus turning like a dog to his vomit.

Rome to London, as it was said, with much seeming humility and lowliness of mind. A considerable company joined together with him, where they had me among them for a little time. The tendency of that spirit was to speak evil of friends that bore the burden and heat of the day, and so to cry out against friends as dead and formal. They expected a more glorious dispensation, than had been yet known among friends; and they kept on their hats in time of prayer. I was but a little while among them, till a vail of darkness came over me, and under that vail, I came to have a light esteem for my dear and ancient friend George Fox, and some others, who had been near and dear to me. But it pleased the Lord to rend that vail of darkness, and cause the light of his countenance to shine again upon me; whereby I came to see the doleful place I was led into, by a spirit that tended to nothing else but self-exaltation, and (under a pretence of humility and self-denial) breach of that unity, love, and fellowship, that formerly we had together, and the good esteem we had one of another in the Lord. Children we were of one Father, esteeming one another above ourselves in the Lord. There was no jar or contention among us then, but all dwelt together in love and unity, and in the fellowship of that blessed gospel of peace, life and salvation.

At my return home from London, I was soon taken to the same prison with my friends in Welch-Pool; and a little before I came among them to prison, the under-jailer dreamed, that he had in his fold a flock of sheep, and that he was wrestling to get in one ram among the sheep, but could not get him in; but when I came to prison, he said to my friend Charles Lloyd, now I have got the old ram in among the sheep. But the jailer turned me out that night to my wife and family; and though I had the name of a prisoner, and was premunired, as the rest of my friends and brethren were for several years, yet I was not kept close prisoner.

This was a time when most travelling friends were taken up prisoners, and though I was a prisoner, yet it lay upon me to get liberty to go and visit friends, in several counties of England and Wales. So I followed my good Guide,* that showed me what to do. I went to the jailer, and told him, I had an occasion to go out a little while, and I could not go out without acquainting him of it, because I was his prisoner. He said, I warrant you will go to preach some where or other, and then you will be taken to prison; and what shall I do then, said he; I told him, that if I was taken prisoner, I would send to him where I was, and he might send for me if he pleased; so he bid me have a care of myself.

In a little time, in the love of God, I took my leave here of my friends and family, and committed myself to the protection of the Almighty. I went to Shrewsbury, and so to Worcestershire, where I had good service for the Lord; so to Tewkesbury, where I was never before. An ancient woman friend followed my horse, and before I had put up at the inn, she was with me, and very cordially said, she had a sense upon her, that I was one of her heavenly Father's children. I went in and refreshed me a little, and asked her, whether she thought I might have a meeting with friends that evening. She readily said, she would acquaint friends of it. And after she had gone a little way out of the inn, she returned again, and desired to know my name, that she might acquaint friends of it. I was straightened in myself to give her my name, though I knew not the cause then; but I desired her to go in the name of the Lord, and if I came in the name of the Lord, they would receive me.

---

* The Spirit of Truth.

So she went, and came again, and told me, I might have a meeting, which was appointed to be at Susan Smithin's; and a blessed heavenly meeting we had, and the Lord gave to us our expected end. There were several professors at the meeting. Some came to me next morning, and discoursed friendly with me about the things of God.

From thence I went through Gloucestershire, where I had good meetings, and so to Bristol. When I was clear of Bristol, the Lord having blessed me, and preserved me so far in my journey, I set forward towards Pembrokeshire. I travelled without any companion but the Lord alone, who was with me all along in my journey; he was my helper and preserver. So I came to the house of our friend Lewis Davies, who gladly received me in the Lord. Staying there some time, they lent me a horse to go to a meeting at Redstone, and I left my own horse behind me, thinking he might rest for some days after my hard riding. When I came to the place, the meeting was out of doors, there being no house, that I knew of, that could contain the multitude of people. When we came to the meeting, Meredith Edwards, whom friends judged unfit to preach the gospel, had the confidence to speak to the people till they were weary of him, and those that were sensible were burthened by him; after some time there stood up a friend and silenced him. I sat as a stranger among them. The Lord was with us, his good presence was our comfort and satisfaction; and after some time I had an opportunity to open to the people those things that belong to their eternal salvation; and having concluded the meeting in prayer, this man, M. Edwards, aforesaid, stood up again and preached to the people, and I turned my back and came away,* and the

---

* Better to turn away, than encourage lifeless preaching.

friends, with most part of the people, followed me. As I was coming out, a friend came and told me, there were two soldiers, (I understood afterwards they were the two sons of a priest) that had brought my horse there some miles. When I saw my horse, I drew nigh to them, and asked them who brought my horse there; they asked me whether I was the man that came from Bristol; I said I was; then, said they, you are the man we look for. I asked them, by what authority they came, or what warrant they had; and they showed me their swords and pistols. I told them, such warrants highwaymen had. Then I asked them, how they durst venture so, among such a company; they said, they knew we were peaceable men, and would not resist: otherwise they would have brought greater force. I told friends, we were not bound to obey them, and desired friends to part, and leave only two or three with me; but friends' love was so great to me, that they kept mostly in a body about me. So I desired the friend to take my saddle and bridle, that was upon the friend's horse that I rid to the meeting on, and put them upon my own horse; so I got upon my horse, and bid them lay their hands off my horse, for I feared not their swords nor pistols; but if they had a warrant from any justice of peace, or lawful magistrate within the county, I would obey it. Then they let my horse go, and I turned a little aside, and saw them lay hold of the other man, M. Edwards; I could not call him a friend, because he was not guided by a right spirit; and I turned myself to them again, and told them, that if any justice of peace, or lawful magistrate within the county, had any thing to say to me that came from Bristol, he should hear of me at the house of William Bateman, in Haverfordwest. I told them my business would require some stay in this country; so they let us go pretty friendly; and I had several brave meetings in

Haverfordwest, and other places in the county. The last I had was at Pontysaison * among the Welsh; they having notice of a Welshman coming to keep a meeting in those parts, many came to that meeting, and good service I had for the Lord, his truth being declared in their own language to them. We had the meeting out of doors, and I stood with my back towards Thomas Simmon's wall of his house. I was young and strong, and my voice was heard to the steeple-house, and most of them came out to hear me; and very few came out with the priest when he had done. When the priest saw such a multitude, he was moved to passion, and would have had the constable take me down. It was reported some said to the priest, they would not take me down, for I preached Christ and the gospel to them, and they would have him come and learn of me himself. I was informed, that the priest's wife and two of his daughters were at the meeting, and were very loving and tender, and came to be convinced of the truth. The Lord was not wanting to us; his life, power, and good presence was with us, and that meeting was the last I had in Pembrokeshire at that time. The friends of that county were very loving and careful of friends, that came from far to visit them. They dwelt in love and unity among themselves. My service was weighty upon me, being myself only without a companion; the Lord alone, that knew the integrity of my heart, was my comfort, support, and exceeding great reward. As for M. Edwards, the two men before-mentioned, took him before a justice; the justice would have been moderate to him, and would have shewed him kindness, but he, by his ungoverned temper, provoked the justice to passion, so that he committed him to the house of correction as a vagrant

---

* Printed Pontchison in previous editions.

for three months, to the great trouble of friends.
I was informed that the justices and magistrates of that county, were generally very moderate in the hardest times of persecution. From Pontysaison I took my leave of friends in Pembrokeshire, and came pretty directly home, blessed be the name of the Lord, to the comfort of my wife and family, and those friends that were prisoners; and the jailor was well satisfied that I came to my prison, without farther trouble to him; there were several taken prisoners, at those meetings I was at, but the Lord preserved and delivered me, blessed be his holy name for ever.

I was but a little time at home, ere John Whitehouse, a follower of John Perrot, came and had a meeting at my house at Welch-Pool. I happened not to be at the beginning of the meeting, but came before it was concluded, and found he had sown an evil seed, and that some of our friends had received it; who soon after joined with that corrupt spirit, which led them to have a light esteem of their brethren, which was a great exercise to many honest friends, and especially to my wife and me; and we were ready to say, hath the Lord sent us here, to be instrumental for a gathering of a people in this country, and hath he suffered the enemy to scatter them in their imaginations. But some time after, the Lord satisfied me, that those who were simp'e-hearted among them, should be restored again into a more settled condition than they had formerly known; and I believed in the word of the Lord. And in time the Lord broke in among them, and opened the understandings of some of them, and they began to reason among themselves, and saw that they were in darkness; so that most of them were restored again into their first love, and lived and died faithful to truth, except Cadwalader Edwards, who continued in stubbornness and hardness of heart, and endeavoured to hurt such who were simple-hearted. I was moved to give forth a paper against him and all his vain imaginations. The following paper was likewise sent to him from friends:

"We whose names are here underwritten, are those that thou hast been seeking to insinuate thy corrupt principles into; and also are those that testify against that seducing spirit that thou art gone into; and most of us do know the terror and judgment of the Lord, for receiving that spirit; and we do exhort all, that they touch not, nor taste of it, lest they be separated from the Lord and his people, and so come under the judgment of the Lord, as we have done; and we have all seen the hurtful effects of that spirit, and in the fear of the Lord, we do deny the same, and them that be joined to it.

Charles Lloyd,	Watkin David,
Richard Evans,	William Lewis,
Owen Jones,	Evan Thomas
Evan Davies,	Richard Davies,
John Reese,	Thomas Hammons,
Elizabeth Lloyd,	Sibil Jones,
Tace Davies,	Katherine Evans,
Ann Lawrence,	Ann Hall,
Katherine Jones,	Sarah Wilson."

This being read in our monthly-meeting for worship, the Lord was pleased to afford us his sweet presence, and his power melted, tendered and mollified our hearts, and caused us to praise the Lord, for his great goodness and mercy to us, in bringing us out of darkness that came over us, by giving heed unto that seducing spirit of John Perrot, John Whitehouse, and

Cadwalader Edwards. And now the Lord having restored us again, we did praise his holy name for the same; and friends were careful afterwards of receiving any spirit that might tend to the breach of love and unity among us. Many other friends brought in their testimonies against that spirit; amongst the rest, one came from our friend Thomas Ellis, who had been particularly warned by me, in the fear of the Lord, not to touch nor meddle with the spirit, though it came with much seeming humility, lest he should suffer thereby; which he did, to his great sorrow, and he set out in his paper and said, this have I suffered for my mongrel moderation: but blessed be the Lord, he was sweetly restored again to his former love and integrity, to the great comfort of himself and brethren.

As to John Perrot, John Whitehouse, and *Cadwalader Edwards, they turned their backs upon God and his truth, and followed the devices of their own hearts and imaginations.

About this time there being a meeting of friends gathered at Aberystwith, in Cardiganshire, most of them were sent to prison to Cardigan, and our friend, Thomas Ellis, was taken prisoner with them. Having the sufferings of these young convinced friends under consideration, I found much love in my heart towards them, even so as to go to the magistrates of the county, to offer myself a prisoner instead of my friend and brother Thomas Ellis, and some others, that that they might go home to visit their families. I acquainted my wife of my exercise, which came pretty close to her; but she likewise in love,

---

* He became afterwards very bad, and ungodly in his life and conversation, and died in the Fleet-prison, at London, being there for debt; yet near his end, he seemed to repent of his wicked life, and told some, 'That they who were preserved faithful among the people called Quakers, would be happy, and that they were the people of God.'

after a little consideration, gave me up for that service. So in a few days I took my journey, and went first to Thomas Ellis's house, to visit his wife and family, before I went farther, his house being about twenty-four miles from Welch-Pool, and not far out of my way towards Cardiganshire. There I very unexpectedly met T. Ellis himself at home; he told me they were all discharged out of prison. Thus I saw it was the good will and pleasure of my heavenly Father to accept of my free-will offering instead of the deed; and my friend T. Ellis and his wife were sensible of my love and kindness to them therein.

And now my service being farther for Pembrokeshire, T. Ellis was willing to accompany me in my journey and we went to Aberystwith, to visit those friends there, where we had a pretty large meeting the first day in the morning, and there came one Thomas Price, brother to Sir Richard Price, of Gogerddan, who took us all prisoners, and committed us to the town prison. That evening we had a meeting in the house where we were prisoners. Many of the town's people, some of them persons of account, were at the meeting that evening. I declared the word of the Lord to them in Welsh, and shewed them the way to the kingdom of heaven. A sweet comfortable meeting we had, and great satisfaction it was to them that were there.

That night a weighty consideration came upon me, about those young convinced friends that were so lately discharged of their imprisonment, because they were like to go so quickly to prison again. So I asked counsel of the Lord, what we might do for, and in behalf of, these young and tender friends; and being under great exercise in my spirit, earnestly praying to God, that he might make some way for their enlargement that time, it came in my mind to write to the chief magistrate Sir Richard

Price, and to give him an account of my journey so far, and that my friend T. Ellis and myself intending for Pembrokeshire, and resting with our friends, and having a meeting with them that day, were taken prisoners by his brother Thomas Price; and if it was his pleasure to send us to prison to Cardigan, that he would be so kind as to leave his neighbours at home, and accept of my friend Thomas Ellis and me, as prisoners instead of them all. To this effect I wrote to him, and sent it next morning; but he sent me no answer. But the high-constable came to us, and told us, we must all prepare to go to Cardigan town, where the county jail was kept. So friends freely and heartily prepared themselves to go. When the time of our going was come, they tenderly taking their leaves of their wives, children, and neighbours, (for some of their neighbours came a little way to see them out of town) the constable stopped, and bid all go home, except Thomas Ellis and me; for it seems the high-constable had private orders not to go with them, but to do as I desired in my letter. Thus the Lord did try those tender friends, and also delivered them.

The constable had instructions to bring us to the quarter-sessions, then held at Lampeter,* and not to Cardigan. When we came there, the justices being upon the bench, we were had before them; some of them were formerly acquainted with Thomas Ellis, he having been in authority, and according to his place, somewhat sharp against offenders. The justices were very moderate to him; but the clerk of the peace was very peevish and froward. I asked the justices, whether that man that questioned my friend, was a justice of the peace; they told me, he was not. Then I told them, we were not bound to answer him; but if they would give me leave, I

---

* Llanbedr in previous editions.

would give them a just account of my business in that county, and upon what account we were sent there before them : and they desired me to speak on. I told them I was at my own house, with my wife and family, at Welch-Pool, in Montgomeryshire, and hearing that my friend Thomas Ellis, and other of my friends, were in prison in this county of Cardigan, for a considerable time, it was with me to come to the magistrates of this county, to offer myself a prisoner, that my friend Thomas Ellis, and the rest of them, might go for a little while to visit their families ; in order thereunto, I came as far as my friend Thomas Ellis's house, where I found him at home with his wife and family ; and they being discharged of their imprisonment, I had a farther concern upon me to Pembrokeshire ; my friend Thomas Ellis, being not willing I should go alone, accompanied me. We came to Aberystwith, to rest there the first day of the week, and had a meeting with our friends, so were taken prisoners, and sent here to you, and now desire to know your pleasure. The justices answered, It was great love indeed, that caused me to come and offer myself a prisoner upon such an account ; and they were sorry Sir Richard Price gave us that trouble to send us there ; and so they discharged us. And the court being silent, I had an opportunity to declare the word of the Lord among them. Very still and attentive they were, as if I had been in a meeting. I commended their great moderation, and in the love of God we parted with then. The deputy-sheriff, and the high-constable that brought us there, came out of the court and treated us very civilly, and would have bestowed on us the best the town could afford, but we were sparing of taking any thing of them. I was informed, that the deputy-sheriff and the high-constable were convinced, and very loving to friends all along. I know not of any that were imprisoned in that county afterwards. The Lord was with us, and he had a regard for the integrity of our hearts, and he alone pleaded our cause, and was with us in our services.

Then we took horse and left the town, and went towards Pembrokeshire, till we came to Cardigan, about twenty-four miles. We met with some hardship on the way, having little or no refreshment till we came here, where we had very good entertainment for ourselves and horses; and from thence we had a friend for our guide towards Pontysaison in Pembrokeshire, but we were benighted, and it rained; our guide lost his way, and we wandered up and down among the peat or turf-pits, and and other dangerous places, but the Lord preserved us out of them all. At length we came to Pontysaison, but it being dark, we did not know the house where our friend, that we intended to go to, lived; but I spoke to our guide to see where the steeple-house door was, and he brought us to it; then I told them, the friend's house was opposite to it; for I remembered when I had a meeting there, my back was against the wall of the house, and my face towards the steeple-house door. So we went forwards and found the house. I desired T. Ellis to call and tell them, that there were some friends that had lost their way, and desired to have lodging there that night. They being in bed, answered, they thought that no good friends were out at that time of the night. T. Ellis reasoned a little with them, but still they were not willing to rise and let us in. At last I called to the friend, whose name was Thomas Simmons, and to his wife, and desired them to rise and let us come in. He asked me, who was there; I told him in Welsh, Richard Davies was there. What, said he, Richard Davies of Welch-Pool? I told them, I was the man. Thereupon the tender, loving friends hastily came down and let us into their house, and we were satisfied in the love of

God. This being the first journey that Thomas Ellis made to Pembrokeshire since he was convinced.

Hence we went to Haverfordwest, and so through all the meetings in that county, till we came to Pontysaison again, and had a meeting there, where there came many friends, both Welsh and English, so that the house could not contain us, and we had the meeting out of doors in the street, and I declared the word of the Lord to them, both in Welsh and English.

As we came to Pembrokeshire, we went to a Baptist's house, and the woman of the house being loving and tender, promised we should have a meeting among the Baptists there. We also appointed a meeting at Newcastle in Carmarthenshire; Peregrine Musgrave, James Lewis, and several other Friends accompanied us to the meeting at Newcastle. The magistrates of the town were very civil, and several of them came to the meeting. The weight and service of the meeting lay chiefly upon upon me; for though our friend T. Ellis was reckoned a deacon, and an eminent preacher among the Independents, yet his mouth was but very little as yet opened by way of testimony among friends. He was an understanding man in the things of God, and was not hasty to offer his offering, till he found a very weighty concern on him. As I was declaring to the people in the Welsh language, I stood opposite to a great window that opened to the street, and there was an evil-minded man in the street that had a long fowling-piece, who put the mouth of it through the window and swore, that if I would speak another word, I was a dead man. But blessed be God, I was kept in that which was above the fear of man, and the Lord kept me in dominion over all. There were two women sitting in the window, and the mouth of the gun came between them both; one of them seeing the gun, turned her back upon it, and said in Welsh, when the man threatened as before, I will die myself first. And there was one in the meeting went to this man, and took the gun away from him, and that wicked man came into the meeting, and was pretty quiet there; the Lord's good presence was with us, a good meeting we had, and I may say, they that trust in the Lord, are as Mount Sion, that cannot be moved. And as it was said of old, as the hills were round about Jerusalem, so is the Lord round about his people, to be a present help to them in every needful time.

Here Pembrokeshire friends and we parted, and it being somewhat late, the meeting having held long, we travelled all night over some doleful hills, intending to be at the Baptist meeting next day, which we had appointed, as before mentioned. It was by computation about twenty-four miles. In this time we had little refreshment for ourselves or horses; but when we came there we had no meeting. The woman of the house said, that the magistrates had heard of it, and charged them, we should have no meeting there. So the slavish fear of man overcame them. The woman seemed to be sorrowful, and would have given us some victuals, but I told her, we did not travel so hard, to come there for her meat and drink, but in the love of God, for the good of their souls.

So here my friend and companion, Thomas Ellis and I parted; he went homewards, and I went that night to William ap Pugh's house, a poor friend, who had a considerable company of small children. I lay on a little straw, upon a hurdle of rods. When the morning appeared, I took a bit of a cake and a cup of clean water, and William ap Pugh and I took our journey towards Radnorshire, which was about twenty miles, mostly over great hills; and when I came there, I staid a little while among friends. Afterwards I hastened home to my family, and when I was come there, Margaret Bowen brought my girl to me, and said, here is a child the Lord hath given thee; she had been sick near unto death. When I was under my exercise in Pembrokeshire, one told me, my child was dead, and my wife not like to recover; which was matter of sorrow to me; and I turned a little aside from friends, and the Lord satisfied me, that neither my wife nor child were dead. When I came home they told me, my child had been as it were raised from death to life. Blessed be the Lord that restored her, and preserved my family, and we were comforted in the Lord.

After this journey I staid a considerable time at home with my family and friends, our meetings were pretty much supplied with travelling friends, especially from the north of England; and though we were prisoners, yet we had our liberty to go to meetings abroad. We had a considerable large meeting at Cloddiaucochion, (the place of my abode) near Welch-Pool, there were at our meeting John ap John,* and James Adamson a north-country friend; but the magistrates of Pool, it being in the limits of their corporation, came and broke up our meeting and took us prisoners. We old prisoners went to the county prison, and the rest to the corporation prison. I took my friend John ap John by the hand, and told him he must come to prison with me; so several of us went together, and when the hurry was over with them, they let us, who were old prisoners, go to prison alone. Then I discharged our friend John ap John, and told him, he should be my prisoner no longer. He staid a little while

---

* John ap John was formerly a hearer of Morgan Llwyd, of Wrexham, and on the occasion of George Fox's visit in 1654, was sent out by the former to try G.F's. testimony. John ap John was then convinced of the blessed Truth, and became very serviceable in the ministry.

with us and then went homewards. The jailer was friendly to us, and after a while I went to the magistrates, and got them all released that night, except James Adamson. The magistrates of the county gave strict charge, that if any north-country Quakers came that way, they should be secured; and I had a great care upon me, to get them discharged as soon as might be: for I knew there was a great concern upon them to visit the churches of Christ wheresoever God sent them. So when I saw a convenient time, I went to the serjeant of the town, and asked him, by what authority he kept my friend there a prisoner; and whether he had a commitment upon him; and he told me, no. Then I desired him to let him come with me, and I would answer for him; so the friend came to my house, and friends and I concluded together, to let him go to Shrewsbury, which was about twelve miles from Welch-Pool; and I desired him to stay there till he should hear from me.

The assizes being there a few days after, the chief magistrate of Pool went, and I went also. And as my friend James Adamson and I were walking under the hall at Shrewsbury we met the magistrate of Welch-Pool, to whom James was a prisoner. He seemed a little angry because I sent the prisoner away, and asked me, how I could answer for it; for, said he, we sent to the Lord Herbert of Chirbury, for a commitment upon him. I told him, they had kept him too long without a commitment, which they could not legally answer. Now he knew not that the prisoner was with me, so I asked him after some discourse, what he would give me for a sight of the prisoner; he considered, and asked me, whether the man who was with me was not his prisoner? I told him he was, for I knew that he was then out of his liberty. So he said to the friend, your friend hath done you and me a kindness; and I see, if there had been occasion, you would have come again; so he parted very friendly with us.

In these times the oath of allegiance and supremacy was tendered to most friends that came into the county, if they were taken, and such were committed to prison, for not taking it, till the next assizes, and then *præ-munired*; and then little hopes of their being released from their imprisonment; and it came to be a saying, and when any Quakers were taken prisoners in Montgomeryshire, there would be no end of their imprisonment.

About the year 1669, my ancient, well-beloved, and dear companion, John ap John, and I, took our journey for South Wales, to visit our friends and brethren in those parts. We went first into Radnorshire, where we had several good meetings. We gave timely notice before-hand, where we appointed the meetings, and several friends and other people came from Herefordshire to meet us at the lower end of the county of Radnor,* where we had a sweet living meeting, and the power of the Lord tendered the hearts of many. We declared the word of the Lord both in Welsh and English. My friend John ap John was very sound and intelligible in the Welsh language. He deserved the right hand of fellowship, for he was my elder, and the first friend that I heard declare in a meeting in the English tongue; and though he was not perfect in that language, yet he had the tongue of the learned, to such who were spiritual. When that meeting was ended in Radnorshire, we both withdrew a little aside from friends, being bowed before the Lord, in a sense of his goodness amongst us. After a little while I turned my face towards the friends, and saw a man coming towards me with much brokenness and

---

* Probably near Kington or Presteign, which towns cannot have been far from the Welsh speaking boundary.

tears; and when he came to me he took me in his arms and held me there. I was very tender of him, though I knew him not. He asked me, whether I did not know him; I told him, I did not; though I said, I could remember something of him. He said, he had cause to remember me. When I looked upon him again, I asked him, whether he was not Roger Prichard; he said, he was the man that had gone astray. And I was glad, yea, very glad, that the lost sheep was found, and that he came to know the true Shepherd and his voice in himself, and he followed Him, and went not astray again, as he did before. He accompanied us to several meetings in that county, and in Mohmouthshire. As we were parting with him, John ap John told him, he had come far out of his way with us. He answered, we had put him in his right way again, and he hoped he should keep in it.

We went through Monmouthshire, and Glamorganshire, visiting friends. We had a good meeting at Scilly, and at Swansea in Glamorganshire: where we met with some French Bretons. We could understand something of their language. We found they were passionate among themselves.

From thence we passed to Carmarthenshire. We had a meeting at Cardiff, and lodged at John Mayo's; his wife Elizabeth was a nursing mother to friends in the beginning. At Cardiff * John ap John suffered great persecution, and in other parts of that country, before I was convinced; I suppose he might be prisoner there in 1653, or 1654.

---

* John ap John was sent to Cardiff gaol in 1655, for asking a question in the steeple-house at Swansea, after the priest had finished his sermon. In the mittimus he is described as of Denbighshire. In 1658 he was several times turned out of Swansea. The reader should recollect that at both these times the common prayer book was not allowed in the parish meeting houses. The Swansea priest was therefore non-episcopal, but no doubt enjoyed Tithes.

We went thence towards Pembrokeshire, where we had several good meetings, and the Lord was with us. Then we came homewards; and before we parted with Roger Prichard, we appointed a meeting at his house, which was at Almeley-Wooton. The Lord helped us on in our journey, and we came there according to the time appointed, and a large, sweet, comfortable meeting we had; I know not that any meeting had been there before. I appointed another meeting to be there; and in a few weeks after my return home, I went accordingly. The concern of that part of the county of Herefordshire was much upon me, and I was often there; and when the people of that village saw me come, they would say one to another, come, let us go to Mr. Prichard's for we shall have prayers there to-night; and the house hath been soon near full of people. A comfortable time we used to have together, and many were gathered to the Lord in those parts. As for Roger Prichard, the Lord blessed him in his basket and in his store, and his heart and house were open to friends, and he built a fine meeting-house at his own charge, and also gave a burying-place, and settled both upon friends for that service, and lived and died in love and favour with God, and in unity with his brethren. "Say to the righteous, it shall go well with them."

About this time I was pretty much at home, and the Enemy and adversary of the growth and prosperity of truth in these parts, stirred up an informer against us, one John David, alias Pugh, a weaver, a tenant to the jailer. We had our meeting in an upper room in the prison, and the said informer dwelt below. Once as he was coming by my barns where my cattle were, he said to some of my neighbours, these cattle are all mine. They asked him, how they were his; he said, Richard Davies had preached three times this day, and that by the laws there is 60l. on the preacher for the same. By this it was noised abroad in the town, that I was like to be undone. My neighbours seemed to be concerned, and one of the aldermen, a relation of mine, came chidingly to me, and asked me, whether I had a mind to ruin my wife and family; could I not leave my preaching, when I when I knew the laws were so severe against us. I told him, I could not, when the Lord required it of me. I desired him to let the informer alone, and let him take his course. He said, he would not; but, said he, I will tell thee what I will do; I will take him along with me to Severn-side, and whet my knife very sharp, and I will cut off one of the rogue's ears; and if ever he informs against thee again, I will cut off the other. I earnestly desired him to let him alone; but he and his neighbours were so enraged against him, that I was afraid they would have done him some mischief.

This informer was a weaver by trade, and the neighbours took their work away from him, so that his children went soon after a begging, many of the town telling them, their father had got a new, rich trade in hand, and that they need need not give them any thing. So the poor children suffered very much; but my wife did not withhold her hand of charity from them.

One time I had my boots on, ready to go out, the jailer, this informer's landlord, seeing him come up the street towards my house, I being in the street, he said to the informer, Mr. *Informer*, you see Richard Davies is going out to preach somewhere to-day, I advise you to look diligently after your business and find him out. If you will not inform against him, I will inform against you. You have got a good trade in hand, and if you do this great service for the king, you must needs have either Dolobran, or Coedcowrid, for your pains. The one was the mansion-house, and the other the jointurehouse that belonged to my friend Charles Lloyd, and his ancestors. Thus the jailer jeered him, and the poor informer travelled great part of that day, from one friend's house to another, to see for me, till he came to Dolobran, where we were met upon church affairs. As we were coming from the meeting, I met him at the door, and discoursed a little with him. He told us, that he was going for a warrant against us to Edward Lord Herbert.

I felt the power of God was over him, and truth reigned among us. He went to the said Lord, and desired a warrant against the Quakers. Lord Herbert asked him, what did the Quakers do; he said, they preached. He queried of him, where did they preach? He told him, they preached at his house, which was their prison. Lord Herbert answered him, let them preach there as long as they will, what have I to say to them? But the informer told him, they met at Cloddiaucochion. He asked whether those there were not prisoners; he answered, they were. Then said Lord Herbert, what do they do at Cloddiaucochion? Do they preach there? He said, no; their way was to sit down, and to look one upon another. He answered, thou art but a fool; the Quakers are a loving people; they went to visit their children, and to eat bread and cheese with them.

So Lord Herbert took his cane, and went from him with his gentleman to walk in his park. The informer followed them, and spoke again to him, and said, will you be pleased to grant me a warrant against the Quakers? He asked him, who sent him there for a warrant? He said, D. Davies. (This was the priest of Welch-Pool, a quiet man, and no persecutor.) Lord Herbert asked him again, whether he had a letter from him; the informer said, no, he thought his word might be sufficient to get a warrant against the Quakers. Upon this, Lord

Herbert, with indignation, it is thought, would have spoiled him, had not his gentleman interposed. He said to him, Is it not sufficient to put my peaceable neighbours in prison? Must I give a warrant to make such a rogue as this is rich, by ruining them and their families? So the informer returned home; and as I was going by his house, he desired me to walk in, as he had something to say to me. I went in with him, and he said to me, I am sorry I did you so much wrong, for I intended much evil against you. I was put on to be an informer, which proved to be mine and my children's ruin; for my neighbours took their work from me, and when my children went to their doors, they would scarce give them any thing to relieve them. And now I desire you to pray to God to forgive me; and I pray you to forgive me also; for I think most of our bishops are Papists, and there is no trust to be put in them. I desired him to have a care what he said, and not lay the fault there; for it was the enemy, the adversary, the devil, that begot that covetous mind in him, against his peaceable neighbours. I desired the Lord to forgive him; and as for me and my friends, we would forgive him; and I desired him to go his way, and to do so no more. So he never informed against us afterwards.

Thus the Lord helped and preserved us through great hardships and difficulties. There was nothing taken from us this time, upon this informer's account.

CHAPTER VI.

PERSECUTION IN MERIONETHSHIRE—PRICE OF RHIWLAS AND SALISBURY OF RUG—D. MAURICE AN INFORMER—HIS MISERABLE END—GEORGE FOX A PRISONER—COUNSELLOR CORBET GETS HIM CLEAR AT WESTMINSTER HALL—THREAT OF COUNSELLOR WALCOTT—LORD POWIS—OPPRESSION OF LUDLOW COURT OF MARCHES—PRIEST OUTWITTED—YEARLY-MEETING FOR WALES SETTLED.

About the year 1675, we heard there was a severe persecution by informers in Merionethshire, especially in Penllyn, near Bala; in which time our meetings did increase there, and many people came to them. A concern lay upon my friend Charles Lloyd and me to visit those meetings, where we had a meeting on the first day of the week at Cadwalader Thomas's, called Wern-fawr. There was abundance of people, more than the house could hold. Two informers came in, and staid all the meeting-time; and after Charles Lloyd and I had cleared ourselves by way of testimony, the people's understandings were very much opened in the things of God, and the way to his kingdom, in the Welsh language, in which I concluded the meeting, the Lord owning of us with his great power and presence, to our great comfort, and the satisfaction of the auditory. The two informers kneeled upon their knees with us, while I was at prayer, and one of them, called Robert Evans, did exceedingly tremble; and when I had concluded the meeting, the said Robert Evans took a paper out of his pocket, and stood before us with much trembling and shaking, and could say nothing to us, but *a warrant, a warrant, a warrant.* Friends stood quiet in the possession of that life and power that God had blessed them withal that day, and we said nothing to him, nor he to us, which was almost an amazement to the spectators; for he was a spiteful, envious man, that had done much spoil upon friends in those parts. At last I asked him, what he had there; he told me, he had a warrant. I desired him to let us see it. He was not willing we should see it; but said, if we would come a little farther on our way, we should see it. We told friends, we were not bound to follow him, and desired friends to depart to their own habitations. But our loving tender-hearted friends would not part with us. Charles Lloyd and I had a great mind to see what the tenor of his warrant was, and who the justices were, that did sign it. So we went along with him to the house where he said we should see it; but the man of the house not being within, he was still loth we should see it. We told him, he should have it safe again, and at last he let us see it; and we saw that Colonel Price of Rhiwlas, and Colonel Salisbury of Rûg, had granted it. We went that night to John Thomas's of Llaethgwn, and were concerned to go and visit these justices. In the first place we went to see whether we could speak with Price of Rhiwlas, to lay the sufferings of friends, that were his neighbours and tenants, before him, for many of them were his tenants; but we could not see him, though we heard he was at home. Thence we went to Rûg, where this Colonel Salisbury lived; and we enquired, before we came to the house, whether he was at home; some told us, he was: but when we came there, they perceived we were those people called Quakers, by our habit and language, and he being conscious to himself what he had done, and what spoil was made upon friend's goods, would not admit us to speak with him. We desired one of his servants to acquaint him, that we had come a great way to visit our suffering friends in that county; and my friend Charles Lloyd bid him tell him who he was; for it seems he was his relation, and an old school-fellow. From thence we went to John ap John's, at Wrexham, in Denbighshire, and visited friends there; and then came home to our families, where we found all things well; and the Lord was with us in our journey.

Some time after this it lay upon me to go and visit friends in London. I went to see the lord Powis and his lady who dwelt then at London, they were my particular friends; and acquainted them with the sufferings of our friends in Merionethshire, by informers upon the late act. They asked me, which way they might be helpful to friends; I told them, if they would be pleased to get a few lines from their brother the duke of Beaufort, then lord-president of Wales, to Colonel Price of Rhiwlas, I did not question but that would moderate them very much: for the said Colonel was not in the main a persecutor, but was put on by some peevish clergyman, so called. In a little time they got his letter for me, with his own seal thereon, but not sealed up; the tenor of it was thus: Sir, I have stopped the complaint of his Majesty's subjects, called Quakers, from coming before the council-board, concerning the severe persecution of the penal laws against them. So when I had this letter, I made what haste I could down into the country, and gave it to a friend and relation of colonel Price's, who delivered it into his own hand. It had good effect; the Lord was pleased thereby to stop the rage and ruin that was intended against friends in that county. The justices of the peace called the informer to an account for what he had done to, and taken from friends, but he could not make up his account. The moderate justices followed him so close, in behalf of the king, that he was near ruined and undone thereby. So it pleased God that himself fell into the snare and evil that he intended against his neighbours.*

Some time afterwards, one Price, priest of Llanvawr, in Merionethshire, was severe against friends for tithes, and some friends came down to me to Welch-Pool with an account thereof. I considered his proceeding upon a *quo minus* from the exchequer, and caused an attorney to appear for the friends, and he, in a few terms, brought me a writ of charges against the priest. When I had it, I was in a great strait what to do with it; for I knew if the priest was taken upon it, it would exasperate him against friends. I sent for some of these friends to be at our quarterly-meeting at Dolobran, which they belonged to. I told them what my judgment was in the matter; and that though there was a writ of costs obtained against the priest, yet it was not expedient to have it executed. I told them, I thought it would be more convenient for them to take the writ, shew it to the deputy-sheriff, and tell him the whole case; but to take care that the writ should not be left with him; which was well approved of, and the friends did accordingly, and kept the writ. The deputy-sheriff knew that would be for the advantage of friends, and was ready to do what he could for them. So he blazed it abroad that the Quakers had got a writ against the priest, and the poor priest was afraid of coming to the steeple-house for several days to perform his service, till he employed somebody to come to friends to make an end of the

---

* The instances were many in which Divine judgment followed informers or savage persecutors, and some of them were very remarkable.

matter: and I never heard that he troubled friends again for tithes while he was there.

About that time that I was at London to visit friends, there sprang up a new informer, whose name was David Maurice, he lived at a place called Pen-y-bont, in Denbighshire, and was newly made a justice of the peace of the county of Montgomery. He that recommended him was informed that he was a sober man, and not given to persecution; but soon after he had his commission, he appeared to be a great persecutor, not only of our friends, but of other Dissenters also.

The said David Maurice, upon the 7th day of the first month, called March, 1674-75, came into a meeting at Cloddiaucochion, with about 14 or 15 persons, most of them armed, where a small number of our friends were waiting in silence upon the Lord. He requesting us to depart, our friend Thomas Lloyd requested of him a quarter of an hour's time before our being dispersed, which he readily granted, and he with his followers sat amongst us. Thomas Lloyd uttered a few words, by way of defining the true religion, and what the true worship was; all which David Maurice approved of as sound, and according to the doctrine, of the church of England; yet notwithstanding, he fined T. Lloyd £20 for preaching, though he was no magistrate of the corporation, and he fined the house £20 and 5/- a-piece for the hearers. And on the 16th of the fourth month, 1675, he caused to be driven from Thomas Lloyd four cows and a mare, all worth about £16 by two of his servants, one of them being his clerk, and the other his tenant, and no officer of the corporation, nor of the parish, nor of that allotment of the hundred, in place with them. These were lurking near the ground about two hours before day, and drove away the cattle before sun-rise, and they were brought out of the county into his own domains.

The same day, about the dawning thereof, the said drivers, by a warrant from the said David Maurice, rudely broke through a neighbour's fields, to the grounds of Thomas Lewis, of Cloddiaucochion, and drove from him six cows, two oxen, and two heifers; alleging for his offence that the said T. Lewis suffered a meeting to be at his house, though the said David Maurice was at the meeting himself, and not only allowed of at the time, but approved what was spoken there.

About the same time Charles Lloyd, of Dolobran, had ten young beasts taken from him by John Jones of Golynog, an attorney at law, who was that year overseer of the poor of the parish of Meivod, together with the petty constable, &c. upon a warrant from the said David Maurice, the only informer and busy justice upon this mercenary act in our borders, for preaching at Cloddiau-cochion, within the liberties of Welch-Pool, the 14th of the first month, 1674-5, though the said Charles Lloyd was not at that place that day, nor many days before or after, at any meeting. David Jones of Branyarth, for being a hearer at the said meeting at Cloddiaucochion, had a brass pan, for his own proper fines, taken from him, and one cow for the pretended inability of others convicted, upon a warrant from the said David Maurice, of Pen-y-bont. But nothing was taken from me, though my family was at the meeting, and I lived within the limits of the corporation.

I being at this time in London, and my service there pretty much in the time of the said hard persecution, my dear friend Charles Lloyd sent me up a full and large account of the sufferings of friends there, by this wicked informer David Maurice; and when I had read and considered them, I was under a great consideration, what way to take to prevent the farther intended mischief of this man; and I laid their innocent and faithful sufferings in secret before the great God of heaven, who hath the hearts of all men in his hand, and may order them as seemeth good to him.

After this, when the time of the quarter sessions was come, the clerk of the peace told the court, he had received the new commissions; which being read, and this D. Maurice being then present, and finding himself left out, he fell into a great rage and passion.

In a little time the said D. Maurice went to London, and was put into commission again; but being made high-sheriff of the county this year, he could not act as a justice of the peace; so he fell into a great rage, for that the said office was like to be chargeable to him. So that year we had peace and quietness; and when his sheriff-ship was over, he was coming through a brook called Lynlleth, near his own house at Pen-y-bont, and it was supposed his horse threw him, and he was carried down into the river Tannat a considerable way, and there miserably perished. Thus the Lord helped us through all our afflictions and troubles: and we see that they that trust in the Lord, shall not be confounded, but are as Mount Sion, and cannot be removed; and as the hills be round about Jerusalem, so is the Lord round about his people; blessed and praised be his holy name for ever and evermore, saith my soul.

In the latter end of the year 1674, I went to visit my ancient* dear friend George Fox, who was a prisoner in Worcester; I passed through Herefordshire, and had some meetings there. I staid with my friend George Fox for some time. He told me how he was taken prisoner, and that he was indicted for refusing the oath of allegiance; that he had been twice removed by *habeas corpus* to London; that he had his trial there, and no error

---

*The word ancient was frequently used for *old* in the 17th century.

being found in his indictment, he was returned back again to his prison at Worcester. As he was opening his case to me, I thought there might be sufficient errors found in his indictment to get him discharged. I told him of a counsellor, Thomas Corbet, a friend of mine, then in London, who was very excellent in finding out errors; so after some consideration, he sent next post for an *habeas corpus*, which came down in a little time, and the sheriff was served with it; so we set forward, G. Fox went in the coach with the sheriff and the clerk of the peace of Worcester, and I rode on my horse along with the coach, and no other friend with us.

We came to London the 8th of the twelfth month, and when we came there, several friends much admired that he should be removed up again; for he was something private in the matter. He desired the friends, who had the management of the business before, to let me have a copy of the record, which was pretty difficult to be had; for several thought it was to little or no purpose; but G. Fox was not satisfied till I had it. I had acquainted counsellor Corbet of the whole case, as far as I could understand it, before I could see a copy of the record; and about the tenth hour in the night, William Mead came with me to counsellor Corbet with it. When he had read it, he said, there were several material errors in it; which put W. Mead to a consideration how that could be; and he desired the counsellor to shew him one error. The counsellor shewed him several errors. W. Mead seemed to wonder that such great errors could not have been found out by other counsel.

The next morning being the 11th of the twelfth month, we went to court, where some other counsellors moved first on G. Fox's behalf, and they were pretty close upon some things, but they knew not of any errors in the indictment. All this while counsellor Corbet was silent. Counsellor Walcott was against G. Fox, and fearing lest they should find some errors in the indictment, he moved, that the oath should be tendered again to G. Fox. Upon which counsellor Corbet stood up and moved, that there was no imprisonment in case of *premunire*. Whereupon the chief justice Hales said, Mr. Corbet, you should have come sooner at the beginning of the term with that plea. He answered, we could not get a copy of the return, and of the indictment. The judge replied, you should have told us, and we would have forced them to have made a return sooner. Then said judge Wild, Mr. Corbet, you go upon general terms; and if it be so as you say, we have committed many errors at the Old-Bailey, and in other courts. Corbet was positive, that by law they could not imprison upon a *premunire*. The judge said, there is summons in the statute. Yes, said Corbet, but summons is not imprisonment; for summons is in order to a trial. Well, said the judge, we must have time to look in our books, and consult the statutes: so the hearing was put off till the next day. As we were going out of Westminster hall, some friends were much troubled, that the Welsh counsellor should start such a plea, contrary to the opinion of the judges, and all the counsellors; and some of them said, they thought G. Fox would have been discharged, if the counsellor had not put in that plea. But honest plain G. Fox said, he had a fine trial, and was cheerful in his spirit. I desired friends to have a little patience, for I thought the Welsh counsellor would stand upon his own legs. So I went to the hall again, and staid for counsellor Corbet till the court was up; and when I found him, I told him, he had started that which many thought he could not make good; and if so, it would be a reflection upon me and the Welsh counsellor, as they called him. He desired me to bring him that evening, another copy of the record, besides what he had. So I got one, and went with it to him; and he writ in the margin something in French, and gave it me again, and desired me to go with it to Thomas Rudyard, who was an attorney in London, for G. Fox, and desired him to deliver it that night to judge Hales, and he would take the other himself to judge Wild; and then he thought there would be little discourse of that matter more: and so it happened.

For the next day they chose rather to let that plea fall, and begin with the errors of the indictment; and when they came to be opened, they were so many and so gross, that the judges were all of opinion the indictment was quashed and void, and that G. Fox ought to have his liberty. Upon which proclamation was made, that if any had any thing to say against George Fox, let them come forth and they shall be heard, otherwise he is discharged. And so he was set at liberty.

Counsellor Corbet, who pleaded this cause, got great fame by it; for many of the lawyers told him he had brought that to light, which had not been known before, as to the not imprisoning upon a *premunire*. And after the trial, a judge said to him, you have attained a great deal of honour by pleading George Fox's cause so in court.

As we were coming out of the court, I had an opportunity to speak to some of London, and to blame them for their unbelief; because they could not believe that any good could come from that plea. I was then of a mind, and still am, that the hand of the Lord was in it, more than the wit and cunning of man; for that trial put an end to all *premunires* in the nation. Our friends, in this county of Montgomery, were most of us under a sentence of *premunire* for many years. Our friend Charles Lloyd was not suffered to see his own house for several years, although it was but five miles from Welch-Pool, where he was kept a prisoner. And as for myself,

I had the name of being a prisoner on the same account for about seven years, but was not kept close prisoner in all that time, but had my freedom and liberty to be at London, and in other places of the nation, as my service was, and as the Lord made way for me. In this time I visited friends pretty much in their sufferings.

So, "good is the Lord, and good is his word, and worthy is he to be praised by all that know him, from henceforth and for ever."

1677. Some years after this trial of G. Fox at London, counsellor Walcott, who was a counsellor against him, was made judge of three counties in North-Wales, viz. Merionethshire, Carnarvonshire, and Anglesey. He began his circuit in Bala, in Merionethshire. He caused several friends to be brought before him, and tendered them the oath of allegiance and supremacy. He did not intend to proceed against them by *premunire*, but said, the refusal of those oaths was high-treason, and he would proceed against them upon that statute for their lives the next assizes; threatening that the men should be hanged, and the women burned. He was a wicked hardhearted man, and intended much mischief to friends, if the Lord had not prevented him. So friends of that county acquainted us here of the whole proceedings in that affair. It being the time that the parliament was sitting, friends concluded, that our friend Thomas Lloyd should go up to London immediately, and we desired him to advise with counsellor Corbet, what to do in the matter, who was then in London. When counsellor Corbet heard of the business, he was much concerned, for he was very well acquainted with this Walcott, and said, by that way they might try us all, if Popery came up again; for they have, said he, the writ *De Hæretico Comburendo* in force, which was executed in Queen Mary's days, for the burning of Heretics, which was not repealed to this day. So counsellor Corbet and Thomas Lloyd went to the parliament-house, and acquainted several parliament-men of it, and that sessions it was repealed ; and judge Walcott was spoken to in London, and our friends were no farther prosecuted, but had their liberty ; and, blessed be the Lord, friends had great peace and quietness in that county for a considerable time afterwards. In a few years judge Walcott died, so there was an end of that persecutor.

In the year 1677, our friend John Burnyeat came to give us a visit in Wales, and had a meeting at Machynlleth, in Montgomeryshire, where appeared an informer, Oliver Maurice, of Drain Llwydion, in Merionethshire, and caused a disturbance, and went afterwards to William Pugh, of Mathafern, near Machynlleth, a justice of the peace for this county, (he was one of them that had his commission when D. Maurice was turned out, as before related page 116) who granted him a warrant ; and himself, together with his bailiff and a constable, meeting John Burnyeat and Thomas Ellis upon the road, stopped them, and seized their horses with their saddles and bridles, so that they were constrained to travel on foot. J. Burnyeat's mare died within an hour and a half after seizure, and Thomas Ellis's horse died in the informer's hands in half a year's time : in which time also a distemper infected most of his cattle, whereby he suffered very great loss ; the said justice likewise fined several other friends at the same time, though they lived in another county. Thomas Ellis dispatched a messenger to me at Welch-Pool, being about twenty-two miles. The next day the Lord Powis being at home at his castle of Powis, I went to him, and acquainted him thereof, and he was very sorry. I desired of him, that he would grant me the favour to make use of his name, that he had heard such and such things concerning the beforesaid justice. Not only so, said he, but let Mr. Edmund Lloyd (this was a neighbouring justice, and no persecutor) write to him, and tell him that I am angry with him for such proceedings. So I went to my friend, that other justice, and got him to write a few lines to the said W. Pugh. So he wrote effectually to him, and I sent it away by night; by which means the rest of the fines were stopped. But John Burnyeat's mare was dead, as before related.

Some time after, there was in this county of Montgomery, one Hughes, a priest, in the parish of Hirnant, where lived a friend, an honest man, whose name was John Rhydderch, who could not pay tithe for conscience-sake. This priest brought several actions against him out of the county-court for tithe; the sheriff's bailiffs drove away several of his cattle, for judgment had out of the county-court. Our friend being well acquainted with the deputy-sheriff, acquainted him of the errors of the proceedings in the county-court; and the sheriff ordered the bailiffs to return the friend his cattle again; so the priest was in a great fret that he lost all that charge. After that, he ordered the friend to be sued at Ludlow court, which was for the marches of Wales. This court was a great yoke and bondage to friends in this dominion; for all answers were to be given upon oath in that court, which friends could not do for conscience-sake. This priest followed the friend with one contempt after another, till it came to a *writ of rebellion*. We let him go on as far as he could go, till the friend was ready to be taken; our attorney gave us an account of it, and I desired the friend to go to a friend's house in Shropshire, which was out of the jurisdiction of that court, and stay there till he should hear from me. I sent to London to John Lloyd, brother to Charles Lloyd of Dolobran, who belonged to the chancery-office, and he sent me down a *prohibition,* and I sent to serve the priest and his attorney with it. The priest fell into a very great rage, and his attorney came to him for seven pounds charge that he laid out for him, but the priest would not pay him; so the attorney sued him, and got judgment against him, so that the poor priest could not go to perform his wonted service for some time. Soon after which the priest died, and I know not whether the attorney had one penny of his money; and that friend was never troubled after on account of that suit.

Our friend Charles Lloyd, of Dolobran, was sued for tithe at the great assizes held for this county of Montgomery, by the earl of Castlemain, impropriator, and Randal Davies, vicar of Meivod, the parish that our friend Charles Lloyd lived in; we were satisfied it was a court of record, and they might sue for treble damage for not paying tithe; so we concluded to go with a copy of their declaration to counsellor Corbet, who lived then at Welch-Pool, and when he read it he said he would demur to it. I asked him whether he could demur in case of tithes? He said, he would maintain a demurrer to that declaration. So when the court sate, he acquainted the judge, that he would demur to that declaration. The judge said, demur in the case of tithe? Yes, in this case, said he. The judge asked him, whether he would demur special or general? Corbet said, when we join in demurrer you may know. So they joined in demurrer; and when it came to be urged, he shewed his cause of demurrer. So the judge and the court were convinced of the error, and they paid cost, and mended the declaration, and next assizes they obtained judgment upon *Nihil dicit.* So Charles Lloyd's cattle were driven for treble damage; but the priest was so perplexed, and put to charge and trouble, that I do not know he ever sued any friend for tithe again.

After this I went to London to the yearly-meeting, and continued there some time, in and about the city, and so came leisurely down through several meetings, visiting friends. A while after I came home, Thomas Ellis and James Halliday came to our town; I told James, it was well done of him to give us a visit in these parts of Wales. They said, they came to visit us against their wills. I asked them, whether they were prisoners; they said, they were: and soon after came other friends with them. I took them along with me to my house to refresh themselves. They told me, James Halliday came from London to South-Wales, intending to take shipping there for Ireland, to be at the half-year's meeting; but the wind proving contrary, he was necessitated to come for North-Wales to Holyhead, and having a meeting in this county near Llanidloes, they were taken prisoners and fined by Evan Glyn, a justice of the peace, and sent here. I was very much concerned for James Halliday, that he should be stopped in these parts, and hindered of his service. So next morning about two of the clock, I took horse and went to this justice's father-in-law, justice Devereux, and found him at a village three miles from Welch-Pool. He asked me, what was the matter: I told him, that his son-in-law Glyn had committed some of our friends to prison to Welch-Pool, and fined them also; and I told him, I thought by the law, that no man was to suffer twice for the same supposed transgression. He gave his son-in-law hard language, and desired me to see some way to get them off. I went to a neighbouring justice, and got James Halliday a discharge, and brought it with me that morning; so we hastened him away with a guide towards Holyhead, and I was informed he had a good and quick passage, and got in time to the half-year's meeting in Ireland, as he intended.

For Thomas Ellis and the rest of the friends, the

jailer took our words, that they should be forthcoming at the next quarter-sessions, at which time Charles Lloyd and myself attended the court, and went to the clerk of the peace, and desired him to call our friends first, which he did. The friends being all at the bar, no prosecutor appearing against them, (justice Glyn being not then come to town), they were soon discharged, without demanding any fees; and after friends had refreshed themselves in town, they went homewards, some of them towards Radnorshire, and those that went towards Llanidloes, met justice Glyn, who had committed them, going towards the quarter-sessions. He spoke to them, and they told him they were discharged. He seemed not to be sorry for it, for he was not a persecutor in the bottom, but was put on by a peevish, proud, informing priest, and I know not that ever he did the like again.

I went to London to the yearly meeting in 1681. Persecution was very severe upon friends in the city, and elsewhere in those parts; at which meeting it lay upon my mind to move for a yearly-meeting in Wales, and after some consideration about it, it was left to friends in Wales to appoint their first yearly-meeting, as in the wisdom of God they should see meet, at their half-year's meeting, held at Swansea the 28th of the seventh month. An account of which my friend Thomas Ellis sent me to London, as followeth:

"Dear Friend, R. Davies,

"IN the love of God is my remembrance of thee at this time, with many others of the like-minded, in and about the city, and especially those who from the beginning have been and still are most exercised under the glorious weight of the care and concerns of the church of Christ; the remembrance of whom hath divers times, and especially of late, as at this present, wrought both eyes to tears, and hearts to tenderness. Although I was disappointed in my expectations of seeing thee here, at this half-year's meeting, yet thy letter to John ap John, coming so seasonably, did so answer for thee, that it was both joy and refreshment to many of us. We had a full meeting of friends from most parts of Wales; many having come upon the account of the yearly-meeting, which was concluded to be at Haverfordwest, the second day of the week, called Easter-week, for the following year. Here were E. Edwards, John ap John, W. Players, Francis Lea, Philip Leonard, and Richard Walter, who had testimonies, and many other friends besides from other remote parts, all zealous for the yearly-meeting. We had meetings here the three last days—.

Thy Friend and Brother,
THOMAS ELLIS."

Swansea, the 28th
of the seventh
Month, 1681.

Thomas Ellis speaks of various Friends *having a testimony*. A "testimony" in such a case means a spoken utterance required by the great Head of the Church and not limited by man or by the will of man. As it proceeds from a Divine source, so it gathers thereto, and baptizes into the name of the Father, the Son, and the Holy Ghost.

Such baptizing teaching is rare; and may be professed, where it is not realized; it is nevertheless a characteristic of the true Church, subject to the exercise of the gift and to being at all times in the will of the Giver.

CHAPTER VII.

BISHOP OF ASAPH TRIES TO GET DISSENTERS INTO HIS FOLD—REASONS WHY QUAKERS DISSENT—R.D. DENIES THE TERM LORD BISHOP AND INTERVIEWS THE BISHOP—LIONEL JENKIN, SECRETARY OF STATE— FALSE BRETHREN—OUTLINES OF SERMON—INSULTED BY QUEEN'S LIFEGUARDS IN 1683.

About the year 1680, or 1681, came Dr. William Lloyd, late of Martin's, in London, to be bishop of this diocese, called St. Asaph.* Persecution was very sharp and severe in several places about this time, upon account of excommunication, and the statute of £20 a month. But this new bishop thought to take a more mild way to work, by summoning all sorts of Dissenters to discourse with him, and seek to persuade them to turn to the church of England. Among the rest, when he came to Welch-Pool, in his visitation, he sent for us. Charles Lloyd, Thomas Lloyd, and myself, sought to speak with him, but I was that day bound for London, so could not, but my friends staid till they had an opportunity with him, and my friend Charles Lloyd gave me an account afterwards of what passed between them, which was to this effect:

That the bishop was much displeased that I was absent; and when he was told of my urgent occasion to go, and my stay on purpose some time to see him, he said, his business was greater, whatever my business was.

---

* For some account of the origin of the diocese called St. Asaph, and of Bishop Lloyd, see Appendix.

That day they discoursed with him, his chaplains, and other clergy, so called, from about two in the afternoon till two in the morning. Afterwards they discoursed with him two days at Llanfyllin.* The first day from about two in the afternoon till night; and the next day, from about ten in the morning till an hour in the night, publicly in the town-hall. The first day at Pool, our friends Charles Lloyd and Thomas Lloyd gave their reasons of separation. In none of the three days would the bishop and his clergy defend their own principles, or refute ours; but only held the three days on the general principles of Christendom, and the apostles' examples of water-baptism, and once a small touch at the bread and wine. Thomas Lloyd held, the last day, our reasons why we separated from the church of England: which were,

1. Because their worship was not a gospel worship.
2. Because their ministry was no gospel ministry.
3. Because their ordinances were no gospel ordinances.

But they would not join with him to prove any of them, though often solicited thereunto; friends being sufferers must submit to all disadvantages: for they had not any notice before-hand of what matters they should argue till they came to the place of dispute, and the last day they forced Thomas Lloyd to about twenty-eight syllogisms, all written down as they disputed, to be answered extempore; and the bishop said, he did not expect so much could be said by any on that subject, on so little warning. And he said, that he expected not to find so much civility from the Quakers; he highly commended Thomas Lloyd, and our friends came off with them very well. They had also much discourse with the chancellor, and one Henry Dodwell, and with the dean of Bangor, afterwards bishop of Hereford, very learned

---

* Spelt Llanvilling in the English edition

men, who were also at the said dispute, with many of
the clergy of the diocese, with some justices of the peace,
deputy-lieutenants of the county, and a great concourse
of people in the town-hall aforesaid, in Llanfyllin.
Several of the clergy, with whom I afterwards discoursed,
seemed not well satisfied with that dispute; for they
said, they thought the validity of water-baptism was
much weakened thereby; and several noted men that
were present said, they thought there could not have
been so much said against water-baptism as had been
said there. It was agreed by consent of all parties concerned, that the dispute should not be printed.

I staid a pretty while in London; and when the Lord
made way for me, I took my leave of the city friends,
letting them understand that I was preparing homewards,
intending for my prison, upon the writ *De Excommunicato
Capiendo*, that was out against me and our friends, and
other dissenters in this diocese called St. Asaph. A
little time before I came out of the city, there came two
or three grave citizens, I suppose of the independent
congregation, and told me, they were come to let me
know that there was a writ *De Excommunicato Capiendo*,
out against me, and there was one of their friends
already in prison on the same writ in our county, and
if I would contribute with them, they said, they knew
how to make it void. I told them, I knew that there
was a writ out against me; and I did also know there
was a friend of theirs, one Richard Trollus, in prison
in Welch-Pool on that writ. I told them, I thought
they might make the writ void, but I would contribute
nothing towards it; for I told them, I would hasten
home as soon as I could, and go to prison if required.
They said, they were satisfied I had other reasons why I
would not make the writ void, and desired me to be free
with them, and tell them my reasons. I told them, I

K

thought they might make that writ void with a great deal of charges; but, said I, how will you prevent the bishop coming on again with another writ which you cannot make void? If there be any error in their proceedings in this, no doubt but the bishop and the chancellor will mend it in the next. And whether do you think it is better for me to go to prison on a false writ, or on a writ you can find no error in? I said, if I go to prison on this erroneous writ, and the sheriff or jailer gives me my liberty, the bishop or the chancellor cannot justly sue them. These men went away well satisfied with the reasons I gave them, and I know of no money they spent to make the writ void.

I acquainted my friend William Penn, and some friends, that I intended to give bishop Lloyd a visit before I went to prison, if the Lord pleased to make way way for me. So my friend W. Penn, the morning before I came out of the city, sent me a letter from the Lord Hide to the bishop, with his coat of arms on it, unsealed. I took my journey and the Lord brought me safe home, to the comfort of my family and friends, who were afraid I had been detained from coming home.

The next morning I set out to see the bishop without interruption; though the sheriff, George Mercer, was very envious to friends, yet I escaped his hands at this time. I went to my friend Tho. Wynne's, who lived in Caerwys in Flintshire, not far from the bishop's palace, and he went with me. When we came there, the bishop's secretary came to the gate. I asked him whether the bishop was within; he said, he was; and asked me, who would speak with him? I told him, that Richard Davies would speak with him. What, said he, of Welch-Pool? Yes, said I. What, said the secretary, my lord bishop! Bishop, as it signifies an overseer, said I, I own; but lord bishop* I deny. So the bishop sent for us in, and there were several clergymen with him, among the rest the dean of Bangor, before-mentioned. The bishop seemed to be dissatisfied that I was not with them at the dispute at Llanfyllin; we went soon to dispute about water-baptism; I told them, there was one Lord, one faith, and one baptism; and that baptism was necessary to salvation; and that water-baptism, which was John's baptism, was to continue and remain but for a season. So this, and such like discourse, held us till it was late that night; and then I went to my friend's house with an order to be there again in the morning. I came in the morning, and we disputed upon the same subject. I said, if one should grant what they desired, viz. that water-baptism was necessary to salvation, which I would not, where should they have an administrator, seeing St. Paul† says expressly, "he was not sent to baptize, but to preach the gospel;" and thanked God that he baptised none, except such and such? 1 Cor. i. 14—17. And Peter, who baptised many, came to see the invalidity of water-baptism that he said, "by baptism we are saved, not the putting away of the filth of the flesh, (outward water could do no farther) but the answer of a good conscience towards God, by the resurrection of Jesus Christ." 1 Pet. iii. 21. They went from this to their Ordination. I put them to prove who sent them to baptize. The dean told me, such an one ordained him; and so named from one to another. I told him, I

---

* A term arising out of anti-christian usurpation.

† It must not be understood that the testimony of Truth committed to the early friends and others since their day, permitted the use of the word *Saint*, other than as there was a conviction of real attainments in holiness in the individual referred to, and to which all are more or less called. Friends usually spoke of "Ives" and "Austell," instead of St. Ives and St. Austell.

thought I should send him to Rome for their succession and ordination. They said, yes, the ordination might be good, though it came from Rome. He brought a comparison; as suppose a malefactor was condemned to die, and a reprieve was obtained, and it came down by the hangman's hand; and though it came so, yet, said he, the pardon was good. Then said I, your ordination comes not by the spirit and power of God.* This return made them somewhat uneasy; and the time being far spent, I was willing to be discharged, having being there part of three days.

I told the bishop of good old David, who said, Psal. xxvi. 6. "I will wash my hands in innocency, so will I compass thy altar, O God; that I may publish with the voice of thanksgiving and tell of all thy wondrous works." Then I said to the bishop, thou canst not say thou wilt wash thine hands in innocency, nor compass the altar of God, while thy writs remain against so many innocent people, willing to suffer till death, for the testimony of their consciences towards God. And I said, bishop Lloyd if I go to prison upon this account, I shall have more peace there than thou shalt have in thy palace. I also said, suppose another prince should arise that would impose something upon thee that thou couldst not do for conscience-sake, what wouldst thou do? He said, then I will go to Pennsylvania also: for at that time many friends were about going there. Then it came clearly to me, and I said to the bishop, though thy head be grey yet thou mayst live to see liberty of conscience in England †; though, as to outward appearance, it seemed to be very far from it at that time.

---

* The thoughtful reader will readily apply this to all whose authority as spiritual teachers comes by the will of man, or as a supposed endowment of grace by the putting on of hands.

† This was fulfilled by the passing of the Toleration Act in 1690.

The bishop called for pen and ink, and said, he would write to the chancellor for my liberty ; but I told him, I was not satisfied for myself to be at liberty, and my friends in prison. So he wrote to the chancellor to suspend the execution of the writ. When he had done, he read the letter to me, and I owned his kindness to us all therein. Then I took Lord Hide's letter out of my pocket, and gave it him. When he saw the subscription, and knew from whence it was, he asked me, how I came by it; I told him, as I was coming out of London, intending for prison, a friend of mine brought me that letter the same morning that I left the city. When he had read it, he said, he hoped I was satisfied that he had granted me the contents of that letter. I told him it was so, and I hoped he would have his reward for his well-doing.

Then I was dismissed, had leave to come home, and brought a letter to John Edwards, chancellor, a peevish man against friends, who lived at Llanymynech, about eight miles from Welch-Pool. When he received the letter, he did according to the bishop's order, and those friends in the diocese, that were concerned therein, were not troubled on that account any more; and the friends that were in prison before, were discharged. We have great cause to bless and praise the Lord for all his mercies, kindnesses, and deliverances to us ; for hitherto he hath been our Eben-ezer; that is, "the Lord hath helped us," 1 Sam. vii. 12.

In the beginning of the year 1682, my dear friend Charles Lloyd and I went to visit friends in Herefordshire, Worcestershire, &c., and came through their meetings to London, before the yearly-meeting. I acquainted my friends George Whitebread, and W. Penn, that I intended to go to Lord Hide, to acknowledge his kindness for his letter, on my behalf, to bishop Lloyd. George Whitehead said, there was some service to be done for our suffering friends in Bristol, and it was thought convenient that three of the city, and three of the country, should go with the said sufferings and desire the kindness of Lord Hide to present them to the king. The three friends for the country were Charles Lloyd, Thomas Wynne, and myself; for the city, George Whitehead, Alexander Parker, and one more. Our friend George Whitehead told me, that our countryman Sir Lionel Jenkin,* (sic) secretary of state, was so cross and ill-humoured, that when the king was inclined to moderation and tenderness to suffering friends, he often stopped and hindered the relief intended them. When we went to Whitehall, we waited a long time before we could speak with them, they being upon a committee a considerable time; but we had sent in by the door-keeper, to acquaint Lord Hide that we were there; and in time they sent for us in. The secretary looked grim upon us. I went to Lord Hide, and acknowledged his kindness for his letter on my behalf to the bishop. He told me that I should tell the bishop, there would be liberty of conscience in England. I told him, I did so; and did believe it would be so in God's time. Secretary Jenkin spoke in a scornful manner, and asked me, what was Welsh for a Quaker; I answered him, Crynwr, Crynwyr; it being the singular and plural number. But the secretary said, we had no Welsh for it, for there were no Quakers in the Roman days. My friend Charles Lloyd

---

* Sir Leoline Jenkins, 1623—1685, was born at Llantrisant, and served in the Royalist army. He acted as tutor in a Welsh family, and in 1662 became Deputy Professor of Civil law at Oxford. Afterwards he entered the Privy Council, and became Secretary of State in 1680; in this capacity he opposed a motion for printing the votes of the House of Commons, and it would appear from R. D's narrative, that he shared the prejudice and persecuting spirit of the ruling powers of that period.

answered, if thou didst ask my friend the question aright, he hath answered thee aright; for there is English, Welsh, Latin, Greek, and Hebrew, for a Quaker. So the secretary said, sir, I understand Welsh pretty well, and English, and Latin, and Greek; but if you go to your Hebrew, I know not what to say to you. I left my friend C. Lloyd to engage with this peevish countryman, and presented Lord Hide with a long list of the names of men, women, and children, in their several prisons at Bristol. I desired him to be so kind as to present their sufferings to the king, which he said he would; and our friend George Whitehead spoke farther to him. Then I turned to the secretary, who directed his words to me, and spoke to him thus in Welsh :

"Mae yn ddrwg gennyf, fod un o Hiliogaeth yr hen Frittaniaid; yr rhai a dderbyniodd y grefydd Gristionogol yn gyntaf yn Lloegr, yn erbyn yr rhai sydd gwedi derbyn y wir gristionogol Grefydd yr awr hon."

The English is thus :

"I am sorry that one of the stock of the ancient Britons, who first received the Christian faith in England, should be against those who have received the true Christian faith in this day."

He replied, he was not against our friends; but, he said, our friends gave their votes for the election of parliament men that were against the king's interest. I told him, it was our birth-right, as we were freeholders and burgesses, to elect men qualified to serve both the king and country; but how they were corrupted, when they came within these walls, I knew not. The secretary would have engaged farther with me in a dispute about religion. I told him, he was an ancient man, and that they had been a long time there upon their business, and if he would be pleased to dismiss us then, and appoint what time we should some morning wait upon him, we would, if he pleased, spend an hour or two with him in discourse about religion, Uupon which he took off his hat, and thanked me kindly for my civility; but we heard no more of him about the dispute. Upon the whole, our friend G. Whitehead told me he was more moderate to friends afterwards than he had been before. The number of prisoners in the list delivered to Lord Hide, to be presented to the king, amounted to, in both prisons, one hundred and thirty-nine; of which there were eighteen aged women, from sixty and upwards, and eight children. In the latter end of the list it was said, "Blessed are the merciful, for they shall obtain mercy."

Friends of Truth allowed any individual, male or female, to minister in their meetings from the gift of prophecy, as might be Divinely required at the time. This precious Gospel liberty was, of course, liable to be abused by forward and unsanctified spirits who were not subject to the openings and shuttings of Him who has the key of David. We find this illustrated in the following account, and later on in the narrative, we find a wrong spirit exposed and confounded though making use of sound words, for those who judge righteous judgment by the unerring Spirit, are not deceived by sounds spoken out of the inward Life.

I had my several exercises this year, 1682, in London, both from false brethren and otherwise. Once I was at the Bull-and-Mouth meeting, and there were in the gallery several troublesome people, and none of our ministering brethren in true unity with us, but George Whitehead and William Gibson. The gallery being pretty full, one of them seemed to strive to keep me out, and our friends G. Whitehead and W. Gibson perceiving it, made way for me to come up to them; another of them had been speaking long in the meeting, and had made many weary of him. I was under great concern in my spirit for the honour and exaltation of the name of the Lord and his truth, and the ease of many that were under weights and burthens; yet, for quietness sake, I silently bore the weight and exercise that was upon me till he had done. Then my mouth was opened in the name and power of God, who had compassion on his afflicted seed, and caused the light and life of his countenance to overshadow the meeting, to the comfort and great satisfaction of the faithful.

I was made to detect the false doctrine, which one of them had delivered to the people, viz. That the children of God are destroyed for want of knowledge. I told the people, that the children of God in these days, were the children of the new covenant; and the covenant that he makes with them is, that "They shall all know him, from the least to the greatest; and the true knowledge of God to his people in these days, is life eternal," John xvii. 3. Though Israel of old were destroyed for want of knowledge, because they forgot the God of their fathers, that brought them out of the land of Egypt, and out of the house of bondage, insomuch that the Lord complained of them, and said, "The ox knoweth his owner, and the ass his master's crib, but my people know not me," Isa. i. 3. And elsewhere it is said, "They have forgotten me days without number." These were those apostates that the Lord complained, Jer. ii. 13, had committed two evils; they had "forsaken him, the fountain of living waters, and hewed them out cisterns, broken cisterns, that could hold no water." These were such as the apostle said, "When they knew God they glorified him not as God, neither were thankful, but became vain in their imaginations, and their foolish heart was darkened. For this cause God gave them up unto vile affections and a reprobate mind," Rom. i. 26. And the apostates in our days, said I, have forgot the God that first made them acquainted in measure with him; so having lost the sense of his goodness, have separated themselves from the love and unity of the brethren; but the children of God, who are faithful to the measure of the grace of God in themselves, know it to be their teacher and leader into all truth. These are not destroyed for want of knowledge, though the world know him not. There are apostates in our age, who have lost the true knowledge of him; but the saints in light have, and remain in the true knowledge of him, being guided by the spirit of truth, whom the world cannot receive, because it seeth him not, neither knoweth him; " but ye know him, for he dwelleth with you, and shall be in you," John xiv. 17.

When I had thus eased my spirit, a concern came upon our friend and brother, George Whitehead, and he sweetly concluded the meeting in prayer.

There was a division in that day among those professing Truth. Sound and faithful friends believed that the same Spirit which had gathered them out of the world's ways and worships also required them to meet together for purposes of church discipline and orderly walking, that their conversation might befit their profession. Others complained that these rules attacked their liberty, and did not see the necessity for all that their more experienced brethren advised, so that some would not be subject to these rules and set up separate meetings. These were less strict against payment of tithes, and in attendance of meetings in times of persecution, but a spiritual blast attended them and they came to nothing.

After this I was pretty well cleared of the city, and was willing to draw homewards. Next first-day I came to Jordans in Buckinghamshire, where we had a blessed meeting; then I had one at Chesham; from thence I went to Robert Jones's near Tring. Thence I went to the quarterly-meeting at Weston-Turfield, not far from Aylesbury, where it opened in me, to advise friends to keep to those rules and methods agreed on among us in our men's and women's meetings. As I was declaring, came in an opposite party; however I went on, and shewed them, how it was agreed among the apostles to send chosen men, endued with the Holy Ghost, to set up good order and method among them. I delivered unto them, that it seemed good to the Holy Ghost, and to us also, to set up our men's and women's meetings that the care and concern of the church of Christ might be upon holy, self-denying men and women, who might take care of the fatherless and widows in their afflictions, and keep themselves unspotted from the world; which the apostle James says, " is pure religion, and undefiled before God," Jam. i. 27. And that the care of all, both poor, strangers, and prisoners in affliction, might be carefully and tenderly looked after, and supplied according to their necessities; and that the ministers of Christ in his day, might take the counsel of the apostle, who said, Acts xx. 28. " Take heed therefore unto yourselves, and to all the flock, over which the Holy Ghost hath made you overseers, to feed the church of God, which he hath purchased with his own blood."

When I had ended what I had to say from the Lord among friends, one of the party stood up, and spoke something by way of reflection, upon what I then delivered. When he had done, our friend Thomas Ellwood proposed to the meeting, that all should sit down, and wait to feel the power of God among us, and let that decide whether I did speak in the name and power of God among them this day; to which the meeting agreed, and all were silent. After which several friends, as they were moved by the Lord, gave tenderly their testimony, that what was delivered that day, was in the name and power of God, and that his presence was with us; as honest Robert Jones, and Richard Baker, who loved the Lord and his blessed truths with all their hearts, and several others present in that meeting. There stood up a young man that I knew not, whose heart was affected, and much broken in spirit, and said on this wise: there is a man come this day amongst us, I know not from whence he came, nor whence he goes; but this I am satisfied, the Lord sent him here, and his power and presence is with him, and his testimony for the God of truth. I enquired afterwards who that young man was; they said he was one John Thornton. Upon this one of the party broke in violently and disorderly against what had been agreed upon among us before the meeting had fully cleared themselves, and finished their testimonies; but it proved greatly to his dishonour and disgrace, so that he was made manifest to those that adhered to him. The meeting held from about ten in the morning, till (as they thought) ten or eleven at night. But blessed be the Lord, that doth not leave his people without a witness to himself; and he is the preserver and defender of all his people that wait upon him. They that trust in him are as Mount Zion, that cannot be moved.

After this I made what haste I could home, taking meetings in my way; at Banbury and the country about, and part of Worcestershire. So, blessed be the Lord, I came safe home to my wife and friends, where I found all things well; blessed be his name for ever.

In the year 1683, I went again to London, to the

yearly-meeting, and staid there some time, after most of the country friends were gone out of the city. I was engaged one first-day for Westminster meeting, and there was no ministering friends present but myself. Several weighty matters opened in me at that meeting, as, concerning the church of Christ, what it was, and on what it was built. I said, some be of the judgment that the church of Christ is built upon Peter; and I opened to the understanding of the people something of what is written in the 16th chapter of Matthew. I shewed them, that which revealed unto Peter, "that Christ was the Son of God," was a manifestation of the Spirit of God in Peter, for it is said, Mat. xi. 27. "No man knoweth the Son but the Father; neither knoweth any man the Father, save the Son, and he to whomsoever the Son will reveal him." God revealed unto Peter, that Christ was the son of God; and he is the only rock that his church is built upon, the rock of ages, the foundation of many generations, that the gates of hell never prevailed against. But the gates of hell prevailed against Peter, when he denied his Lord and Master in the time of his sufferings; and therefore he was not like to be the rock which Christ built his Church on. It is said, 1 Cor. x. 4. "For they drank of that spiritual Rock that followed them, and that Rock was Christ." So Christ is the sure foundation that his church is built upon. Peter saith, 1 Pet. ii. 5, &c. "Ye also, as lively stones, are built up a spiritual house, an holy priesthood, to offer up spiritual sacrifices, acceptable to God, by Jesus Christ." And in verse 8, he acknowledged Christ to be the Rock. Paul saith, 1 Tim. iii. 15, that "The house of God, the church of the living God, is the pillar and ground of the truth." This, said I, may inform the blind and ignorant of this age, that lime and stone, and temples that are built with hands, are not, as they say, the church of

Christ, and the house of God; "for God dwelleth not in temples made with hands," as saith the prophet Isaiah, lxvi. 1, and the martyr Stephen, Acts vii. 48. Thus I was concerned to declare the truth in that meeting, with much more to the same effect. After meeting I went with some friends towards the city; and as we were coming along the Strand, the Queen was going from her chapel, and some of her life-guard were very rude, and with the staves they had in their hands, they did knock and beat friends that had their hats on,* all along as they came. I received a blow upon my head, so that it swelled, and was sore for a considerable time. But blessed be the Lord, in all our exercises and afflictions, his life, power, and presence bore us up in the midst of them all; praises be to his pure and holy name for ever.

---

* This violent, and unseemly behaviour, arose from friends' faithfulness to their testimony against hat-honour. Why should the head be uncovered as a sign of reverence or honour to any mortal, be it King or Queen? The Queen being a Catholic, probably her body-guard were of that faith.

CHAPTER VIII.

R. D. BY MEANS OF INWARD GRACE AND DISCERNMENT DETECTS A JESUIT PREACHING AS A QUAKER— RENEWED PERSECUTION FOR ABSENCE FROM THE CORRUPT NATIONAL WORSHIP—THE DECLARATION OF INDULGENCE—COMING IN OF THE PRINCE OF ORANGE— KINDNESS OF THE THEN BISHOP OF ASAPH—SCHOLARS AT OXFORD ATTEND MEETING IN 1706.

Before I came out of London, we met with more exercises and troubles. One first-day in the morning, I was not well, and could not go to the meeting, nor scarcely get out of my bed; but when the time of our afternoon meeting came, it lay upon me to go to the Bull-and-Mouth; and I told Job Bolton, with whom I lodged, that I must go to the said meeting. He reasoned with me; but I told him I would go so far as I could; and he said he would go with me. As we went through the passage to go in, I heard a voice that I was satisfied was not the voice of a true shepherd, the meeting being already gathered, and many people there. When I went up to the gallery, one was preaching of perfection, who said, "Be ye perfect, as your heavenly Father is perfect," &c. I staid to hear him but a very little while, till I stood up and judged him, and told the people, that the kingdom of God stood not in words, but in power, righteousness and holiness. Then this man went in a rage out of the meeting, and a considerable company followed him; and a friend or two went after them as far as Fleet Street, to see where they were oing; and one of the company saw the friend, and desired him not to follow them too close, lest they should do him a diskindness. We heard afterwards, there was a wager laid that this man, who some said was a Jesuit, would preach in the Quaker's meeting, and he should not be discovered; and had he gone without reproof, they would say, that a Jesuit preached in a Quaker's meeting, and they could not discern him. But it was reported at many places in the city, that he was detected in the Quaker's meeting, and he could not abide there. We have cause to bless the Lord for his goodness to his people, that gives them a discerning spirit to judge between good and evil, and between those that serve God in truth and righteousness, and all deceitful hypocrites, who are to be judged and condemned by the word of his power.

In the beginning of the year 1685, king Charles died, and king James came to the throne, and the statute of £20 per month for absenting from the public worship, which I suppose was made against the Papists in queen Elizabeth's days, had been and was very much put in force against our friends, whereby many of them were almost ruined; the sheriffs and their bailiffs prosecuted them so severely, and did make such a prey of them, that some worth many hundreds, were made so destitute, they had scarcely a bed to lie upon, but were robbed of all. When king James came to be settled upon the throne, our dear friend G. Whitehead, who always was much concerned for the sufferings of friends up and down in the nation, and who did not spare himself to visit kings and parliaments, and all others, where he thought he could get relief for his suffering brethren, went to king James, and laid the present condition of suffering friends before him. After some consideration, the king told him, that what concerned him, or came to him of those fines, he very freely and readily would remit. Upon which an order was granted, to suspend the rigour of their prosecutions. But it seems, when it came out, the Roman Catholics took the advantage of it to themselves; which was some surprise to friends who had laboured in that service. George Whitehead hearing I was in the city, came to me, and told me the whole business, and understanding that I had interest with the Earl of Powis, who was great with the king, he thought it might be of service, if I would go along with him to the Earl.

Next morning my friend G. Whitehead and I went to the Earl of Powis' in Lincoln's-inn-fields. When he understood I was come in, he very soon came to me; and when I had ended my country business with him, I told him I wanted a little of his advice in a case wherein our friends were great sufferers by a law that was made against them, and that we were severely whipped upon our backs by the statute of £20 per month,* for not coming to hear that which is called divine service. I told him that a friend of ours had waited upon the king, and had told him the whole state of things, and that the king was very ready to relieve us in what he could, and that an order was granted to that purpose; but it seemed his friends had taken the benefit of it, and ex-

---

* By this Statute (23 Eliz.,) Friends in various parts of the country suffered severely. It provided "that every person not repairing to Church according to the Statute of the 1 Eliz. 2, shall forfeit twenty pounds per month, for every month they so make default," and Eliz. 29 provided that "the Queen may seize all the goods and two-third parts of the lands and leases of every offender not repairing to church as aforesaid * * * so long as they shall forbear to come to church."

These infamous statutes had probably more of a political than a religious origin, and were intended by means of an external uniformity in religion to induce greater subservience to the government.

Happy it was for England that Divine goodness raised up a people who steadfastly opposed such cruel and oppressive mandates, and suffered cheerfully the spoiling of their goods and frequent loss of personal liberty until honourable relief came.

cluded us,* &c. I desired his advice, whether we should proceed farther in it or no; he answered, by all means; for, said he, I will tell you, that there was taken from our friends in Lancashire, £8000 upon this statute, and the king and myself went to see how much of this money came into the exchequer. When we saw it, it appeared that the king was in debt to that account about £28, and all the rest gone. I desired him, seeing it was his advice that we should go on, and not be discouraged, that he would be pleased to grant that a friend of mine might come in and speak with him, who was more able to give him an account of this business than myself, and who had been to the king to get relief in this matter; for G. Whitehead stayed all this while in an adjacent room; so he bid me bring him up to him. When George came, he opened the matter fully to him. When he thoroughly understood the matter, he soon got himself ready, called for his coach, and bid me come to him at an appointed time; and he brought an absolute order from the king, to stop all proceedings by sheriffs and bailiffs upon that account in the nation. In a short time the rage, envy, and cruelty of such devouring men were stopped, and I know not that any have been troubled or suffered since upon that statute. Blessed be God, that hears the cries of the poor, fatherless, and widows, and sends relief to the afflicted in his own due time. I must say, that the Earl of Powis and his countess were very ready and willing at all times to do our friends any kindness that lay in their way, and to help them out of their troubles and afflictions; and I am apt to believe they did it conscientiously, for there were many of our friends in

---

* There is little doubt that King James was much more tolerant at heart than others of his religion who would have influenced state affairs prejudicially, had not the Revolution of 1688 prevented them.

several of their lordships' hereaways, and the Earl never suffered any of us to be fined for not appearing in any of his courts upon juries, or any other way or manner.

In the year 1688, it seemed good to king James to publish a declaration for liberty of conscience, and ordered the bishops to send it to their several dioceses, that it might be read. Seven of them would not read it. Bishop Lloyd aforesaid was one of them, therefore they were committed to the tower. Then I remembered that which I spoke to the bishop at his palace in the year 1681, when I queried of him, what if another prince should arise, that would impose something upon him that he could not do for conscience-sake? And that year when at London, I went to visit him in his troubles; and he said to me, I have often thought of your words, and I could wish I were in Pennsylvania now myself. He told me the reason why they could not read the declaration, saying it was arbitrary, and not according to law, and that it was a matter of conscience to them; and others were to have their liberty by it, besides Protestant Dissenters. He told me also, that they were put on to do those things which they had done against Dissenters; but when I told him of it before, he could not believe it, till it came thus upon them. I had acquainted him formerly, that I had read a sermon that was preached to prove the church of Rome to be a false church, because she was a persecuting church; and now, said I, the members of the church of Rome put you on, not only to persecute upon the penal laws that were made against Dissenters, but by those laws also that were made against Popish recusants: and by the same argument may we and they say, the church of England is a false church, because it is a persecuting church. The bishop said, they did not consider nor know it then as they did now. I took my leave of him, and he kindly acknowledged my visit; and after some time they were released.

Afterwards the bishop came to Welch-Pool, in the assize week, and in the evening sent for me to the high-sheriff's house; there being with them most of the justices and deputy lieutenants of the county, with many of the clergy, who were very civil to me. The bishop told them that he had sent for me, and that he was more beholden to me than all the men in the diocese, for I came to visit him in his troubles; and he desired of them to do me all the kindness they could, and he would take it as done to himself. When supper was over, the bishop and the high-sheriff, Edward Vaughan, of Llangedwin, took me into a private room with them, and we discoursed a little about the times. There was some report of the coming in of the Prince of Orange, and in a little time I had an account that the prince was landed, which was great satisfaction to the bishop; for he said some prosecuted him very close for his life. And when the Prince of Orange was made king of England, &c., and liberty of conscience was established by law, he and others were well satisfied with it.

And now I think it worthy to take notice of the several kindnesses, upon account of our suffering friends, I received from this bishop Lloyd, in his several dioceses; for as we record the hard-heartedness and cruelty we have found from unmerciful persecuting bishops and clergy, and how many they have made widows and fatherless, I think it is justice and equity in us to record all the mercy, tenderness, and compassion, we find

---

* A teachable Bishop—would that all those who have since occupied the seat of Kentigern were as willing to learn, and come as near confessing that the church of England is a false church.

from those that are conscientious and charitable among them.

Bishop Lloyd being at a visitation in Llanfyllin, in this county of Montgomery, four peevish men, churchwardens of Welch-Pool, did intend to prosecute my son-in-law, Jacob Endon, for not paying towards the repairs of their worship-house;* I went with my son-in-law, and waited on the bishop, and told him the case; he very quickly called the church-wardens, and told them there was an act of parliament ordering a more easy way, and with less charge, to recover by distress, than to drive to excommunications. He inquired for the act, which I gave him; and he turned to that clause, read it to the wardens, saying that he himself drew that clause in the act, and told them how they ought to go to the justices for a warrant; but, said he, why will you go to the charge of a warrant? Cannot you go and take a pewter dish, or some other thing near the value? I warrant they will never sue you for it; for, said he, we must do unto them, as we would be done unto, if we were in their condition; so he quickly dispatched them. Then I told him, I was come moreover in the behalf of a prisoner on the same account, whose name was Richard Davies, near Ruabon, in Denbighshire; and he advised me to go to the chancellor, Dr. Wynne, whom I should find, he said, a very fair man; so he called him to us, and left us together; and I took my leave of the bishop, acknowledging his kindness. When I had fully discoursed the chancellor about the prisoner, I found him very fair; and in a little time after, I heard my friend R. Davies was discharged; and several kindnesses I had of the chancellor since. When the said wardens came home,

---

* *Worship-house* or *meeting-house* is a more correct and Christian name for what is commonly called a church. In the New Testament bricks or stones are never called by the latter name.

they reported what favour I had with the bishop, and were troubled thereat; but neither myself nor son-in-law were ever after troubled about those repairs of their worship-house.

Another time when I was going to London, and visiting friends in my way, I called at Timothy Burberough's, at Aino-on-the-Hill, in Northamptonshire, where I understood he was gone to prison. I inquired the cause of his imprisonment, and his wife told me the priest of the parish had left their small tithes, and other tithes, till he thought they amounted to a considerable value; and then he came and took away nearly all they had, and sent him to Northampton jail, where he had been for some time. I took a memorandum of it, and when I went to London, I thought of the affliction and exercise of my poor brother. My old friend bishop Lloyd being then at London, I went to his lodgings at Whitehall, and I must say, he was very ready to come to me. After some discourse, I laid the distressed case of my friend T. Burberough before him. He answered, he did not know what to do in it, the priest of Aino was a stranger to him, and out of his diocese. I told him, if he would be pleased to write a few lines to the bishop of Peterborough, for it was in that diocese, I said, he might peradventure write a few lines to the priest of Aino, to be more moderate and conscientious, in not taking more than the value of that which he called his due, and casting the poor man from his family into prison also. The case I left with the bishop, and he took care to send it to the bishop of Peterborough, who sent it to the priest of Aino; and bishop Lloyd sent the priest's answer, with a letter from the bishop of Peterborough to himself, in a letter of his to me near Welch-Pool; which I took as a great kindness and favour from him.

Not long after this I went to London again, and

called at my friend T. Burberough's, where I found him at home, being released; he told me the priest had sent an order for him to come home: and that he came to reason and discourse with him. It seems he was not so unkind as he had been formerly.

In the year 1700 there was a considerable suffering on friends in Worcestershire, an account of which was given me by my friend Edward Bourne, of Worcester, who desired me to use my interest with bishop Lloyd* for the relief of John Fowler, and his mother-in-law, the widow Banbury, who was a prisoner for tithe in the out county prison in Worcester, and he sent me their whole case. When I understood it, I found a concern upon me to make what haste I could to the bishop, who was then at his palace at Hartlebury, a few miles from Bewdley. I considered also what a great sufferer our friend William Sankey had been by one Vernon, a cruel ungodly priest of the parish he lived in, who had cast him into prison, when he had five or six small children, and his wife lately dead. He several times took from him more than treble the value of his pretended due for tithe. From Bewdley I went to William Sankey's, and told him I was to go to the bishop, and desired him to go with me. In the morning we went together. I inquired for the bishop's secretary, Francis Evans, who very lovingly came to us, brought us in, and said he would acquaint his lord that I was there; and in a little time the bishop came to us.

And after some discourse I told the bishop, I was not only come to give him a visit, but I was come purposely from home, in behalf of some friends of mine, who suffered for tithes in that country; and that I was informed there had been three committed to Worcester jail by one Kerry, the priest of Tredington, and that two of them were released, and the third remains a prisoner.

---
* Then Bishop of Worcester.

Released, said he, how are they released? I told him, by the hand of their great Creator. It seems then, said he, they are dead; and the same man, said I, doth prosecute the widow of one of them, viz. William Banbury's, and hath already put her into your court, for that which her husband suffered and died for; and we reckon that in common law, when the prisoner dies in prison, the prosecution ceases. I do not know, said he, but the debt may be paid, but the charges are not; and I know not what to do with that man, for I hear he is a very covetous man, and I have no power over him but once in three years. I was lately in my visitation there, and had I known this then, I might have done your friends some kindness. I said, if thou wilt be so kind as to write a few lines to him, and let him know what complaint is made to thee of him, and how thou art informed that two of the three which he sent to prison are dead, I do not question but it might stop his rage and severe prosecution against the poor widow, if not be a means to release the other prisoner. So he bid his secretary take notice of it, and put him in mind to write to him.

Then I told him of the sufferings of William Sankey, who was there present, and desired him to give my friend leave to open the case himself to him, which he did; and when he said how cruel the said Vernon had been to him in casting him into jail, his wife being dead, and left five or six small children; and he told him, he had taken from him goods worth about £12 for about £3 or £4 demand for tithe; and about £12 or £14 worth of sheep, for the like demand at another time; and several other cruelties he had done him by this unconscionable Vernon. The bishop taking it into consideration, caused his secretary to draw an order for him to come there with his accounts, that was due to him from W. Sankey, and what he had taken from W. Sankey towards that account; and he gave the order to William Sankey, to deliver to the priest, and desired William to be there the day appointed, with the priest. I was informed the priest went the day before to the bishop, and W. Sankey went the day appointed; and I was informed that the bishop should say, there was no help for what was past, but he would take care he should do so no more to William Sankey. I heard since that time he hath taken it in kind from him, with more moderation than before, and that the bishop was kind to W. Sankey ever since.

John Fowler, one of the three before mentioned, (Robert Grimes and W. Banbury being dead) was discharged; and as for the widow Banbury's case, who was severely prosecuted by the priest, intending to get it to an excommunication, that was stopped, and she was troubled no more.

Before I parted with the bishop, I told him, there was a friend of ours, William Cattrill, that kept school at Worcester, who was prosecuted very close by some, for keeping school without a licence,* and they did intend to bring him under an *Excommunicato capiendo*, and if he was not pleased to be kind to him, they would put him to all the charge and trouble they could. The bishop bid his secretary take care about it. So all that I requested of the bishop at that time was friendly and kindly granted me, and care was taken that they were not troubled nor molested on these accounts. Then the bishop ordered us to dine there that day, and we parted friendly and lovingly with him; and he desired me when I came that way, not to be strange to him. From thence

---

* This is another illustration of the extraordinary arrogance of the National preachers of that day. Education of the young they considered a perquisite of their own, or to be under their control. Hence, a qualified teacher keeping school without a licence, was liable to prosecution.

I went to Worcester, and gave friends an account of my success with the bishop. I staid with them a little while, and then went to Bromyard, and had a meeting there. So I went through part of Herefordshire to Leominster, and I can bless and praise the name of the Lord, who was with me all along on my journey, and brought me safe home to my wife and family; and when I gave them an account of my journey, they praised the Lord with me, who had been my preserver and defender.

In a little time after, I went to London, and being at the meeting about friends' sufferings, there was mentioned the sufferings of friends in Lancaster castle by the dean and chapter of Worcester, and they had been there for several years, though friends had made interest to get them off, and friends at Worcester used their interest with the chancellor, who seemed to be very kind to them; yet for all that they could not have them discharged. When I came from London I went to the bishop at Worcester. He was very free with me, and in a little while the chancellor came to us, and the bishop gave me to understand who he was. I told them I was glad to see them both together, and said, when I was lately in London we had the sufferings of our friends in Lancashire before us, for a small matter of tithe, alleged* to belong to the dean and chapter of Worcester: and I told the bishop I thought the chancellor was not a stranger to it, for I had heard he had been often solicited on their behalf. The chancellor told him, he did under-

---

* Reader, mark the word *alleged*. R. D. does not acknowledge that the dean and chapter had any true claim for tithe. What the law allows is one thing—what truth, justice, and the fear of God allow is often something different.

It is wrong for a man to support a form of religion which conflicts with the testimony given him by the Father of Spirits to bear, and any law which gives others access to his property on that account is an unrighteous law.

stand it, and that these men were there for a small inconsiderable matter: and said, he was sorry those men died in Worcester, because in conscience they could not pay that little tithe* to the priest of Tredington, and he was afraid these men would die there also, unless some way was found out for their release. The bishop asked how long they had been there; I think the chancellor said four or five years. The bishop said, discharge them, discharge them; and ordered them to be discharged without paying any fees. After a little time I parted with the bishop and chancellor, and acknowledged their kindness. I went to friends in the city of Worcester, and told William Pardoe what success I had with the bishop, desired them to wait on the chancellor to get the order, that it might be sent speedily; and in a little time 1 heard they were discharged.

---

* To pay three pence in tithe, would be as burdensome to an enlightened conscience, where the nature and effects of pure Christianity were manifest, as would a payment of thirty pounds. In fact long and tedious imprisonments were sometimes endured for refusal to pay very small sums.

CHAPTER IX.

APPOINTED TO MEET QUEEN ANNE AT WINDSOR—THE SCHOLARS AT OXFORD MANIFEST SOME IMPROVEMENT—ATTENDS YEARLY MEETING AT LONDON—LAST ILLNESS AND DEATH.—TESTIMONY OF GEORGE WHITEHEAD AND OF THE QUARTERLY MEETING.

The autobiography of R. D. ends with the preceding chapter, but the narrative is continued by another hand thus:—

Hitherto, reader, thou hast had a short relation of some of the labours and services of our ancient and honourable friend Richard Davies, from his own account, which he finished a little before his decease; it remains therefore, to give some account of his last year's travels, together with the time and manner of his departure &c.

In the year 1702, he went to London, his daughter Tace Eudon accompanying him, and stayed in and about the city several weeks, visiting friends in their meetings, and had many good and comfortable opportunities among them. He, together with eleven friends more, were appointed by the yearly-meeting to go to the queen at Windsor, with an acknowledgment from friends for the continuation of their liberty and protection under her government; at which time he in particular spoke to the queen. When he was clear of those parts, he returned homewards, and came through Worcester, where he went to visit his old friend bishop Lloyd, who was glad to see him. That was the last time they saw each other.

After his return home he often visited some neighbouring meetings, and was at the yearly-meeting of Wales the spring following.

About the latter end of the third month, 1704, he went up to London again to the yearly-meeting, his grandson David Endon attending him. He visited friends as he passed through Stourbridge, Banbury, Aylesbury, &c., and stayed in and about the city for nearly two months, being somewhat weak and sickly. When he was clear of the city, he returned pretty directly home and came well to his family.

In the beginning of the year 1705, he met with some exercise; for on the 1st of the third month, his dear and honest wife died, who had been very tender and careful over him, and a woman very serviceable to friends and truth in many respects. She was a plain, upright, and honest-hearted woman; one that loved truth in simplicity. She left a good report behind her, after they had lived together about forty-six years.

In the first month, 1706, he was at the yearly-meeting of Wales, Llanidloes, in Montgomeryshire, being the last yearly-meeting he was at in Wales. On the 15th of the second month following, he took his journey with his grandson D. E. towards Bristol. He had a meeting at Leominster, and at Ross in Herefordshire, and thence went to Bristol, and lodged at Charles Harford's, junr., where he visited friends at their yearly-meeting, and stayed about a week; and on the 30th of the second month, set forward towards London, and came to French-hay, and had a meeting there. The 1st of the third month he had a meeting at Sodbury in Gloucestershire; the 5th at Cirencester; the 8th at Oxford, being the first day of the week, where many of the scholars came in, and were rude for some time; but after our friend Richard Davies had spoke a while in the meeting, they became more sober; some of them sat down, and stayed till the conclusion of the meeting; and friends took notice that the meeting was much more quiet than usual.

I may here remark that the opposition of the "scholars" of Oxford and Cambridge to the spread of Truth was very marked, on several occasions, between 1654 and this date. In 1654, one woman friend lost her life in consequence of severe ill treatment from these educated ruffians, which resulted in a contusion in the side (see Besse's sufferings).

It is to be feared that at the present moment, although outwardly more civil and restrained by better laws, that a knowledge of religion as a life in the soul is lamentably rare at the older universities, perhaps even more so among those of them who are professedly training to become the spiritual guides of others.

So long as religion is looked upon as a means of livelihood, and of attaining social position, whether among Episcopalians of the national stamp, or dissenters, this must be so, and the kingdom of Christ cannot come with power to the nations.

When people's minds are turned inward to the Pearl hid there, and to the Anointing within, "which is no lie," the beauty of Christianity will shine forth as never before, and they will look with abhorrence upon those systems of the night of Apostacy, which kept them in a ministration of the letter at the hands of a carnal, man-made ministry, instead of directing them to attendance on the great Minister of the Sanctuary before whom all flesh must be silent.

The narrative continues:—

From thence he went to Henley, and had a meeting there; and so to Windsor, where he had a meeting; thence he went to London, and lodged at his friend and kinsman's Thomas Lloyd's. He attended the yearly-meeting, and staid in and about the city, visiting friends at their meetings, until the 19th of the fourth month; at which time he returned homewards, and had a meeting the 21st at Chesham where William Bingley was; the 22nd they had a meeting at Aylesbury; and thence went to their yearly-meeting at Banbury, where were many friends from divers parts. The 28th he came to Worcester, William Bingley still accompanying him, where they had a meeting. The 30th he went to Droitwich, and had a meeting there. The 1st of the fifth month he had a meeting at Bromsgrove; the 2nd at Birmingham, and lodged at John Pemberton's: the 4th he went to the quarterly-meeting at Wolverhampton, and passed thence to Stourbridge, and lodged at Ambrose Crowley's; and so upon the 9th of the fifth month, 1706, he returned safe home to his family at Cloddiaucochion, near Welch-Pool, having been away nearly three months.

After this journey he continued mostly at home, in his usual health, and visited several neighbouring meetings. In the latter end of the eighth month, he was at the burial of an ancient* woman friend, Anne Thomas, in Salop, and at several other burials near home; at which times he often had very good service, and people would hear him gladly, for he had a solid and grave delivery, and was wise and sound in his matter, which was very taking with most people.

His last sickness was very short; for on the sixth day of the week he was at Welch-Pool, and finding himself

---

* Ancient is here equivalent to "elderly."

not well, went home, and the next day kept the house. On first-day following several friends went to see him from Dolobran meeting, and had a little opportunity to wait together upon the Lord with him. He spoke very little to any; and his pain continuing upon him, the next day, being the 22nd of the first month, 1707-8, about the ninth hour in the morning, he quietly departed this life, being in the seventy-third year of his age.

The 25th being the day appointed for his burial, many friends from divers parts, and other people, met at his house at Cloddiaucochion, and his body was borne by them to the grave-yard, near his own house, and there decently interred near his wife's grave. In the grave-yard there was held a solemn meeting, and several testimonies were borne, in the power and life of truth, to the general satisfaction of the people.

It was a frequent practice when the memorials of a deceased friend were presented to the world, for some of those who had best known the departed to give forth written testimonies to the work and character of the one who had passed away. I have not here reprinted the whole of these, but believe that the following will be instructive.

George Whitehead was one of the most prominent early friends, and his active service covered the long period from 1652—1722; if I am not mistaken he had interviews with Charles II., James II., William III., Anne and George I.

Being turned when quite a youth to the inward grace and light, by the powerful preaching of George Fox, and some of his early coadjutors, he stood like a rock during the whole of that long period, and fervently laboured in word and doctrine, in imprisonments and trials, not a few, until he became a pillar in the spiritual temple which should go no more out.

As we look back on Richard Davies' narrative, we may note one characteristic in its unadorned, unaffected simplicity; even in the testimony the eulogy is measured and moderate, yet we don't discount it in our minds, we accept it as a just and enlightened estimate of a good man.

THE TESTIMONY AND ACCOUNT OF GEORGE WHITEHEAD, CONCERNING RICHARD DAVIES AND HIS MINISTRY.

In a true and living remembrance of this our dear brother, ancient and faithful servant and minister of Jesus Christ, Richard Davies, and of that dear and brotherly love that remained between us, and which he had to all faithful friends and brethren in Christ, I am concerned to give this brief testimony in commemoration of him, his life, and faithful gospel ministry.

He was not only a professor of the name, power, and spirit of our blessed Lord and Saviour Jesus Christ, but also made a partaker of Christ, in spirit, life, and conversation; a plain, meek, and humble man of integrity; a man fearing God, and hating iniquity; a man sanctified by the Holy Spirit, unto unfeigned and constant love of his brethren in Christ; a man sound in faith, in patience, and charity; of a sound mind and judgment, being endued with the spirit of love. He was a preacher of Christ and his righteousness, in his conversation as well as in doctrine and ministry, wherein he was exemplary to the believers, &c. He was given up to serve the Truth and friends; and being of a tender spirit, did truly sympathize with the sufferers for the same, and used his industrious endeavours for their relief, where he could have an interest or place with such as had power.

His testimony and ministry was evangelical, plain, and sound; not in words of man's wisdom, but in the demonstration and plain evidence of the holy spirit and power of Christ, being a minister of the spirit, and of the New Testament; the new covenant dispensation, which stands not in legal shadows, types, outward signs or figures, but in the gospel life and substance, even in Christ Jesus; in whom all the shadows, and dispensations thereof, are ended.

And this our dear brother having travelled through and beyond those outward dispensations, shadows, and vails; and understanding their cessation removal and end in and about Jesus Christ, his sufferings and death; and more especially by his inward and spiritual appearance, dispensation, and work in his heart and soul; whereby he was made sensible of the power of Christ's resurrection, as being one risen with him; by the brightness and glory of whose day, the shadows naturally vanish and flee away; as this faithful minister of Christ was witness, with many more of his brethren, who were and are partakers of the inward and spiritual revelation of the mystery of Christ, and of the glory of his day.

And as this gospel minister did see and partake of the enduring substance, and end of all vanishing shadows and carnal ordinances, he well knew, that neither John's baptism with water, nor any outward washings therewith, though once commanded, could ever sanctify, or wash the inside from sin and pollution, or sprinkle and purify the conscience, or make a true Christian; much less can sprinkling infants, which God never commanded; but Christ's spiritual baptism, and washing of regeneration by the water of life, which is the one baptism, *i.e.* the baptism of the spirit; this is the only saving baptism, as our said deceased friend hath testified, according to holy scripture.

He also likewise testified, that outward bread and wine, cannot feed nor nourish the immortal soul, or inward man, any more than the legal passover; but only the body or outward man: but Christ, the living bread, the bread of life, which comes down from heaven; and the cup of blessing, which he gives to his spiritual communicants; he being that spiritual meat and drink, which all his spiritual Israel partake of, in this his gospel day, to their great refreshment and comfort, in the spiritual communion, and comfortable fellowship of his Holy Spirit. And to this our dear friend's ministry tended to bring people, that they might not rest in lifeless shadows, but come to know and inherit eternal life and substance in Christ Jesus, which all that truly love him shall partake of and possess.

And I am fully persuaded, that as this our dear and well beloved friend and brother lived and died in the faith, in our blessed Lord and Saviour Jesus Christ, and in true union and communion with his church and people here on earth; so I believe he is eternally blessed, and at rest in his heavenly kingdom; where all the faithful in Christ shall meet in the great and generally assembly of Christ's triumphant church, and enjoy glorious and everlasting communion in the heavenly kingdom of glory and peace; which shall be the blessed estate and inheritance of all who continue faithful in true love and unity, in the grace of God, while here on earth, unto the end of their days.

London, the 10th of the
Twelfth Month, 1709.

G. W.

A Testimony from Friends and Brethren of the Quarterly Meeting from Montgomeryshire, Shropshire, and Merionethshire, held at Dolobran in Montgomeryshire, the 25th of the Eleventh Month, 1708, concerning our ancient, honourable Friend and Elder, Richard Davies.

He was one of the first of friends in these parts, who received the blessed truth in the love of it; and he laboured much in the morning and heat of the day.

He and his wife were very hearty, loving, and ready to entertain friends, their hearts and house being very open in that respect; and they were very helpful and serviceable to friends in this country, who were prisoners on truth's account in Welch-pool, the place where they then lived, where there were but few other friends of ability to assist them; until the Lord raised up several eminent instruments in these parts, who were very serviceable with them.

Our said friend was wise and prudent. He had a good understanding and capacity; a man of great experience; and was very willing to advise and counsel any in things relating to the gospel, and also to outward affairs.

And as he was discreet in his conduct among men, the Lord gave him great place and favour with several persons of note, with whom he had often good service for truth and friends.

The Lord blessed him with a good gift in the ministry, and he was made an able minister of the gospel; sound in judgment, and well received by most people who heard him.

He travelled pretty much in divers parts on truth's service, especially in his younger years; and had good service in many places where his lot was cast, both at home and abroad. He was often at London, where he was well esteemed by many of our elders and brethren.

He lived to a good old age, and was favoured with a short sickness at last. Some of us were with him the day before his departure; he seemed sensible that his end was near approaching, and appeared as one that was waiting for the same. He departed this life the 22nd of the first month, 1707-8, in the 73rd year of his age; and we believe he is at rest with the Lord, together with many more of the faithful followers of the Lamb.

We shall not enlarge much farther, but refer to the ensuing* account of his labours, travels, and services for truth and friends on several occasions, which contains a general relation of the most remarkable occurrences and passages of his life, which was written by himself not long before his decease.

And we earnestly desire that all, who make profession of the glorious truth with us, may really know "a working out of their salvation with fear and trembling;" and that they may faithfully improve their talents in their age and time, and truly follow the examples of the faithful elders and servants of the Lord in all things wherein they followed Christ, that we may give our account at last with joy, and receive an eternal reward with the faithful children of the Lord, when time in this world, to us will be no more.

So, " Blessed are the dead which die in the Lord, from henceforth; yea, saith the spirit, that they may rest from their labours, and their works do follow them." Rev. xiv. 13.

Signed on behalf of the said meeting, by us,

Charles Lloyd,	Owen Lewis,	Edward Ellis,
Owen Roberts,	Tho. Cadwalader,	William Soley,
Rowland Owen,	Richard Lewis,	Richard Benbow,
William Reynolds,	John Richards,	Griffith Owen,
Robert Vaughan,	Ellis Lewis,	Richard Ruff,
Humphry Owen,	William Osborn,	John Roberts,
Robert Griffithes,	Thomas Oliver,	Julias Palmer,
Jacob Endon,	Joseph Davies,	John Kelsall,
John Simpson,	Richard Evans,	Amos Davies.

---

* Originally prefixed to Richard Davies' Memoirs.

APPENDIX A.

John ap John and Francis Gawler.

The following Extracts from "Besse's sufferings" may prove of interest—they illustrate the history of the times as well as the Christian character of those concerned to withstand the ruling powers.

A.D. 1655, John ap John being in the steeple-house at Swansea, in Glamorganshire, after the minister had ended his sermon, asked him whether he was a minister of Christ. This question gave great offence not only to the priest of whom it was asked, but also to another of the same function then present, who discovered his wrath by instantly seizing John by the collar, and without suffering him to speak another word, dragging him out and delivering him to a constable who confined him that night in a close dark prison.

Next day he was brought before the magistrates, whom the priests laboured to incense against him, requiring in their fierce zeal to have him whipped, that the devil might come out of him, and as often as he attempted to speak, one or other of the priests would strike him and stop his mouth with their hands. At length he was sent to prison by the following mittimus, viz:

To the keeper of the common gaol for the County of Glamorgan, or his deputy at Cardiff.

Where as it hath been proved by oath before me, that John ap John, of Denbighshire, hath misbehaved himself contrary to the laws, and security being therefore by me required for his personal appearance at the next great sessions, to be held for the said county, hath obstinately refused to the same. These are therefore, in the name of his Highness the Lord Protector, to charge and require you forthwith to receive into your custody the body of the said John ap John, and him safely in your goal to keep and retain, until he shall give good security for his appearance at the first great sessions, and in the meantime to be of good behaviour toward his Highness, and all good people of this nation; and hereof fail not, as you will answer the contrary at your peril. Dated at Swansea under my hand and seal the 8th day o October, 1655.

ROBERT DAWKINS.

Francis Gawler of Cardiff, was several times imprisoned for his testimony against the corruption of the priests. At Cardiff he was hauled out of the steeple-house, shamefully abused by the people, and violently struck by the priest himself with his cane. At another time, for asking the priest a question, after his sermon before the judges, he was committed to prison, and detained there many months. He was also again imprisoned for a long time for speaking to the same priest in the street. In the steeple-house yard at Landaff, he and Alice Burkett were greviously abused, where the said Alice was stoned, and had her clothes torn off her back, and the priest's wife struck the said Francis so violently with a key, that he felt the blow a long time after. At Swansea, as he was standing still in the steeple-house, hearing the priest, he was suddenly assaulted, dragged out, and imprisoned in the Town-hall, though his behaviour was peaceable and quiet, nor did he say anything. But his religious concern to testify against the priests of those times being well known, so exposed him to their resentment, that they stirred up the people by abusing him, to prevent his uttering such reproof as their own consciences told them they deserved. Hence it also happened, that he was frequently carried before the magistrates, and by them dismissed for want of any colourable pretence to proceed against him.

The said Francis Gawler, Edward Edwards, and Elizabeth Holmes, being taken in a meeting in Shire-Newton, were brought before John Nicholas, William Bleathin, and Robert Jones, justices of the peace, whose examination of them before many people present at justice Bleathin's house, was as follows, viz

Justices. You have broken the law in meeting together under the tree so near the Church, and we have several times warned you of it before this, therefore we must deal with you according to the law.

Answer. We have broken no law of the nation in meeting together, for the law of the nation giveth liberty to all to meet together in the faith of Christ, in which we met together; therefore we have broken no law.

Justice Nicholas. The law saith, the minister should not be disturbed, going to or coming from his exercise.

Answer. That law we have not broken now, for we did not see the minister, nor speak to him.

Justice Nicholas. Though you did not see the minister, nor speak with him, yet you know he was disturbed by your meeting, being in the way so near the Church, where the people did go forth; so by this there was a disturbance.

Answer. We believe the minister and you were troubled, because the people came forth of the steeple-house to our meeting, yet we have not broken the law, for the law saith, it must be proved that such came wilfully, maliciously, and of set purpose to make disturbance; and if such an oath were taken before thee, we think thou wouldst hardly believe it.

Justice Nicholas. We shall do nothing but what we

have proof for. Some did hear the voice of one of you in the church, and so it must be a disturbance.

Answer. It must be proved, that such an one did maliciously and wilfully make a disturbance, therefore let it be proved.

Justice Nicholas. Walter Jenkins' voice was heard in the church, and therefore it must be a disturbance.

Answer. Walter Jenkins was not here this day; therefore believe them not who inform thee against us.

Justice Nicholas. Walter Jenkins was here the last time, and his voice was heard then.

Answer. That which thou dost question us for, is meeting together now, and that we have made a disturbance, which cannot be proved. What Walter Jenkins did is past, and he is ready to give an account for what he has done.

Justice Nicholas. Do you own the Scriptures to be the true Word of God, yea or nay?

Answer. If thou sayest the Scripture is the Word of God, prove it, and produce one Scripture that saith, the Scripture is the Word of God.

Justice Nicholas. I will do so.

Justice Jones. We will not prove it till you first deny it.

Answer. It lies upon the Governor to do it, whether we deny it or no, because he said he would prove it, therefore let him.

Justice Jones. We shall not prove it, till you first deny it.

Answer. The Governor said, he would prove it, so we may refuse the answer till he proves it; yet notwithstanding, for the sake of the simple-hearted people here, if you will take an answer according to the Scriptures of Truth, we shall answer you, which we know may satisfy you.

Justice Jones. We are willing to receive an answer according to the Scriptures of Truth.

Answer. The Scriptures we own to be the words of God, which are a declaration of the Word of God, which was from the beginning, before the Scriptures were written, and is as an hammer and a sword, dividing asunder between the marrow and the bones, and to this the Scripture stands a witness for us. John i. 1, 23. Heb. iv. 12.

Justice Nicholas. You have given us more satisfaction than some of your friends have done, and you speak very well, to own the Scriptures to be the words of God, which indeed is Truth, and we are glad to hear you.

Justice Jones. But how is it you call our ministers deceivers, and some of you never saw their faces before, which is a strange thing to us, I pray you tell us.

Answer. It is an easy thing to know a deceiver and a false prophet, for they are marked with the mark of the beast in their foreheads, and you may read in the Scripture, so many hundreds were marked with the mark of the beast in their foreheads, and they were those that upheld the worship of the beast in their idols' temples, where the beast is now worshipped in this generation, by which mark the false prophets are known to be the deceivers, though their faces we never see; and take heed how you uphold them, lest you be partakers of their plagues.

Justice Jones. Indeed, we read in Scripture, as you say, that so many hundreds were marked with the mark of the beast in their foreheads, but it is a strange thing to us, that you know our ministers by that mark.

Answer. We believe thee, friend, where thou art, that it is a strange thing to thee; but if thou wilt come down to God's witness, the light which shines in thy heart, thou wilt come to see it, as plain as we speak it.

Justice Nicholas. Yea, but do you not know, that you have profited by our ministers, and that the presence of God went with them? I pray you honestly confess.

Answer. We shall honestly declare unto thee. There was a time that the presence of God went with some of them, and in that time they did bear witness against tithes, types, figures, and shadows, saying, Christ was come, and has set an end to tithes; and some of them durst not receive them for conscience sake, the which now they receive and plead for, and receive hundreds by the year by it; therefore the presence of God is withdrawn from them, whom we deny, and by their fruits they are known.

Justice Nicholas. We will let them alone to plead for themselves.

Answer. Do so, and let them fight for their God; and our weapons shall not be carnal, but spiritual.

Justice Jones. You say, the light shines in the heart, which gives the knowledge of God in the face of Jesus Christ, and in so doing you add to the Scriptures.

Answer. We say, the light shines in the heart, which gives the knowledge of God in the face of Jesus Christ, and if thou deniest it, it lies upon us to prove it.

Justice Jones. Yes.

Then F. Gawler turned to 2 Cor. iv. where the text being plain against the Governor's assertion, he honestly confessed his error before the people, saying:

Justice Jones. You are in the right, and we are mistaken.

Answer. We shall not make thee an offender for a word, but if thou hadst such advantage against us, thou wouldst hardly have past it by, but we are taught to do so. Thou and the Governor have asked us many questions, and you cannot say you are dissatisfied in any one particular. Now we would ask you one question, did Peter and Paul speak one thing, and mean another when they spake?

Justice Jones. Nay, they did not speak one thing, and mean another.

Answer. Then do not thou make meanings to their words.

Justice Jones. I shall not do it.

After their examination, they were detained some time in a neighbouring alehouse, and then by the justices order set at liberty, having had an opportunity in the alehouse to declare the truth to the people who followed them from the justices, and heard them with much attention, being much satisfied with what they had heard at the time of their examination at the justice's house, where the room was full of people.

APPENDIX B.

The Diocese of Asaph (Llanelwy).

The opening events of Chapter vii. are of an unusual and interesting character.

We find the supposed spiritual head of the diocese "called St. Asaph," as Richard Davies rightly expresses it, actually having a conference with dissenters to win them back to the fold of the Church of England.

I may be permitted now to make a digression, and allude to the origin of the said diocese. Early in the fifth century, in the troublous times immediately preceding or accompanying the withdrawal of the Roman power from Britain, a strong contingent of Britons from the district between the Solway and the Firth of Clyde, left their homes to seek, through force of arms a more peaceful asylum in Wales. They succeeded in occupying that part of North Wales which stretches from Chester to Barmouth. More than a century later, when heathenism had to some extent succeeded in re-establishing itself in Strathclyde, a Christian preacher named Kentigern had to escape from his country and passing southward came to the British territory spoken of above; he was well received and given land in Flintshire, by the banks of the river Elwy where he established a religious community, which was reputed to contain 965 souls. That it was a monastery in the modern sense of the term I much doubt, the time of those in the community was taken up with agricultural education, religious exercises, or going on missionary tours, and the settlement was called Llanelwy, a name which it bears to this day.

Nominal Christianity was restored in Strathclyde, and

Kentigern, was invited back to Scotland by Rhydderch Hael; he left as his successor at Llanelwy, a certain Asaph about whom little is known. From him comes the English name of the place. The diocese called St. Asaph nearly corresponds with the British settlement of Cunedda, the leader of the North country Britons.

Kentigern, after returning to the North was very active in propagating a form of Christianity, and some parish meeting-houses even in Aberdeenshire are associated with his name.

His other name Mungo, is simply a compound of the Welsh *mwyn* and *cu*, which might be translated *gentle and beloved*; we may take it that this was his real character.

The crypt of Glasgow cathedral is supposed to hold his ashes.

Dr. Wm. Lloyd, 1627-1717, was of an Anglesea family and born in England was regarded as of puritanical tendencies, and strongly anti-papal. He favoured the advent of William Prince of Orange, and afterwards obtained the See of Worcester. His consideration to dissenters, contrasts very favourably with the stand-off haughty spirit which some would-be spiritual pastors display.

www.ingramcontent.com/pod-product-compliance
Lightning Source LLC
Chambersburg PA
CBHW020248170426
43202CB00008B/272